The Story of Europe

H. E. Marshall

The Story of Europe

The present edition is a reproduction of previous publication of this classic work. Minor typographical errors may have been corrected without note; however, for an authentic reading experience the spelling, punctuation, and capitalization have been retained from the original text.

ISBN: 978-1-64799-949-0

PREFACE

MANY European histories written for school use are too long for careful study by young pupils during the necessarily limited time allotted to the subject. Many of them are overloaded with details of battles and domestic politics which, although of importance in the thorough study of one country, have little or no influence on the general growth of Europe. It is very important that students should realize as early as possible that the history of our islands has at all times been influenced by the broader movements of European history, and in this book an endeavour has been made to give, succinctly, the main factors which have gone to the forming and developing of the various European states from the fall of the Roman Empire to the Reformation, together with sufficient detail to enliven that dullness which is the almost inevitable accompaniment of great compression.

As a good deal of time is generally devoted to the history of England in the ordinary school curriculum, it has seemed unnecessary to enlarge on it here. The history of England has therefore rarely been touched upon save when (as in the Hundred Years' War, for example) that country plays a prominent part in the politics of Europe. On the other hand, considerable space has been given to the period immediately following on the fall of the Roman Empire, that being a period somewhat neglected, but which yet gives the necessary key to future developments.

To aid smooth reading the dates have been for the most part relegated to the margin. In the case of rulers the dates of the beginning and end of their reign have been given; of all other personages those of birth and death.

CONTENTS

THE BARBARIANS INVADE
THE ROMAN EMPIRE

IN the first centuries of our era the one great power of the world was Rome. All southern Europe bowed beneath the conquering sword of the Romans. Africa and Asia, too, owned their sway. For the Mediterranean, the great trade route of the then known world, was theirs, and the countries bordering upon it became mere provinces of Rome. Even the uttermost islands felt their might, and sailing beyond the "narrow seas," Cæsar set his hand upon the island of Britain. From the Rhine and the Danube in the north, to the desert of Sahara in the south, from the borders of Wales in the west, to the Euphrates and the Tigris in the east, the empire stretched.

Of this wide empire Rome was the capital. Secure upon her seven hills she sat, mistress of the world, a city without rival, until in A.D. 330 the Christian emperor Constantine the Great resolved to build a new Rome upon the shores of the Bosphorus. Constantine called his new city New Rome. But men did not take readily to the name, and the capital upon the Bosphorus became known as Constantinople, or the city of Constantine. It is difficult to-day to remember that Constantinople was founded by a Christian, and was at one time the bulwark of Christianity against the Turk.

The Romans called themselves lords of the world. And so it seemed they were. All the trade and skill, all the art and learning of the known world, were theirs. Beyond the borders of the Roman Empire the world was given over to wild barbarians, who were skilled neither in the arts of war nor of peace. That the civilization of Rome should go down before their ignorance seemed impossible. Yet the barbarian triumphed, Rome fell, and the mighty empire crumbled into dust.

"Rome was not built in a day," neither did Rome fall in a day. The fall was gradual, and came both from without and from within.

It came because there was tyranny in Rome, and no state can long be held by tyranny and the power of the sword alone. The high officials and tax collectors cared nothing for the people's good, they cared only for gold.

1

They laid heavy and unjust taxes upon the middle classes. These classes must always be the backbone and support of a nation, but in Rome's last days they were so oppressed that they ceased to exist. The backbone of the nation was gone. So when wild barbarian hordes poured over the borders of the empire Rome fell.

When the Emperor Theodosius died, about sixty years after the founding of Constantinople, he left two sons, both mere boys. They divided the empire between them, Arcadius, the elder, taking Constantinople for his capital, ruled over the Eastern Empire, and Honorius, a child of eleven, became ruler of the Western Empire, with Rome as his capital. It was upon Rome and the Western Empire that the full force of the barbarian onslaught fell.

First came the Goths. These were Teutons or Germans, and were divided into two tribes, the Visigoths or west Goths, and the Ostrogoths or east Goths. They were tall and strong, their eyes were blue, their hair long and fair. They were lawless, greedy, and treacherous. They came at first fleeing from the Huns, a far more barbarous foe, seeking shelter beneath the still all-powerful sceptre of Rome. They found the protection they desired, but ere long they turned their swords against the men who had provided it.

The March of Alaric

Under their young king Alaric, the Visigoths attacked the empire again and again. Twice Alaric laid siege to Rome. Twice he spared the imperial city. Still a third time he came, and this time he sacked and plundered it without mercy. Then, laden with rich booty, driving a long train of captives before him, he turned southward. The proudest city in the world lay at his feet, and flushed with victory, he marched to invade Africa.

But an even greater captain than the conqueror of Rome met him on the way. Death laid his hand upon the victorious Goth, and all his triumphs were blotted out. The new king of the Goths, Ataulphus son of the Wolf, did not follow up Alaric's triumphs. He turned aside from Africa, forsook the wasted plains of Italy, and marching his war-worn followers into southern Gaul and northern Spain, settled there.

Meanwhile other barbarian hosts attacked the outposts of the empire. For in a vain endeavour to guard Italy and Rome itself the last

2

legions had been called back even from Britain, and the northern boundaries of the empire were left a prey to the barbarians.

Over the wall which stretched from Forth to Clyde stormed the Picts and Scots, across the Rhine and the Danube poured wild hordes of Franks, Burgundians, Lombards, Allemanni, and Vandals. The Franks settled in Gaul, and made it Frankland. The Burgundians, too, settled in Gaul, and to-day the fair province of France lying between the Loire and the Saône still keeps their name. The Vandals settled in Spain, of which a province is still named Andalusia (Vandalusia). The Lombards, or Longbeards, overran northern Italy, and to-day the central province of northern Italy is still named Lombardy. Angles and Saxons left their homes on the Weser and the Elbe, sailed across the sea, and taking possession of southern Britain, changed its name to England.

Every one of those barbarian tribes which thus rent the Roman empire to pieces was of German or Teutonic origin. And from the ashes of fallen Rome a new Teutonic empire was to arise. But meanwhile a foe far more fierce and terrible than any German tribe, was sweeping onward ready to grind to dust the already crumbling empire. This foe was the Hun.

Attila and the Huns

The Huns were a warrior race coming from out the wastes of Asia. They were small and swarthy, their eyes were dark and piercing, their noses squat, and their hairless, hideous faces were covered with frightful gashes and scars which made them more hideous still. They spent their lives on horseback, and rode so well that they almost seemed part of their sturdy little ponies. With much riding, indeed, their legs were so bowed that they could scarcely walk. They had no houses, and few possessions. They neither ploughed nor reaped, but lived on raw flesh and clothed themselves in skins. They were fierce, blood-thirsty, vile, and all men fled before them with a shuddering dread.

These were the people who, now led on by their mighty king, Attila, made Europe tremble. Of all the Huns Attila was the most terrible. Though small of stature, his shoulders were of great breadth, and there was something of kingly authority in his piercing, evil eye and loathsome, scowling face. Where he passed he left desolation behind him, and gloried in it. "I am the curse of God," he boasted proudly, "the hammer of the world. Where my horse's hoofs have trod the grass will grow no more."

3

Like a devastating flood the Huns swept over Gaul, leaving behind them a track of blood and ashes. Town after town was given to the flames, and the fair fields were laid waste. Then, at length, forgetting their old quarrels, Roman and Goth joined to crush the common foe. The Goths, under King Theodoric, and the Romans under Aëtius, "the last of the Romans," marched northward. Franks and Burgundians, too, joined the army, and upon a plain near Chalons a great battle was fought between the allies and the Hun.

The struggle was long and fierce. Theodoric, king of the Visigoths, was slain, but in the end the Huns were defeated. Defeated they were, but not crushed. Like a wounded animal behind the rampart of his baggage wagons, Atilla crouched, growling and watchful. So dangerous he seemed that the allies dared no more attack him, and content with their victory, they marched homeward.

This fight has been called the battle of the Nations. And although the victory was not a decisive one, a great question was settled upon the field of Chalons. There it was made plain that Europe was to be the heritage of the Christian Teutons and Romans, and not of the pagan Mongols.

Attila was too crippled to renew the fight, and sullenly he recrossed the Rhine. But the following year, having gathered another army, he marched through Italy, leaving, as was his wont, a trail of ruined cities and devasted plains in his wake. Rome was his goal, but ere he reached it his course was once more stayed. For, accompanied by certain nobles, the pope, Leo I, came out to meet the savage conqueror.

Upon the banks of the River Mincio the misshapen heathen met the priest of God. Upon the one side there was religion and knowledge and everything that stood for civilization, discipline, and lofty aims. Upon the other there was ignorance, licence, and base lust of blood.

Leo came unarmed to meet the foe before whom all Europe cowered. Yet he conquered. His solemn words of pleading and warning pierced the heart of the fierce heathen. Perhaps, too, the gold which he brought in his hand as a bribe from the feeble emperor aided not a little the eloquence of his words. However that may be, Attila yielded. "Hastily," we are told, "he put off his habitual fury, turned back on the way he had come, and departed with the promise of peace."

"I can conquer men," he said, "but the Lion (Leo) knows how to conquer me."

4

In this appeal made by Leo the Great to a heathen foe we see the first beginnings of the enormous power in worldly matters which the popes of a future day were to wield. But other arguments besides those of the bishop of Rome hastened Attila's going. For "the Huns were stricken by the blows of heaven," famine and pestilence thinned their ranks. So, taking the gold which was offered to him, their leader returned, perhaps not unwillingly, to his own borders. He hoped doubtless to come again at another time to wreak his will upon Rome. But the following year he died. His empire fell to pieces, and the Hun vanished from Europe.

THE RISE OF THE FRANKS

IN the beginning of the fifth century the Franks were among the many tribes of Teutonic origin who helped to dismember the Roman Empire. They took possession of part of Gaul, which, in time, became known as Frankland, and which formed the nucleus of the state which we know to-day as France. When the Franks invaded the Empire they did so in a manner different from that of the other Teutons. They did not cut themselves off from Germany. They did not wander far into the Empire, making conquests now here, now there. They simply crossed the border, and taking possession of a small portion, settled there.

Nor were they like the Goths and Vandals a single people who marched to war in a body. They were made up of various tribes who moved about independently of each other and who settled in various places. Their great strength lay in the fact that they kept their line of communication open. While plundering the Empire they still kept in touch with the great unexploited forces of the heathen world behind them.

The chief of these Frankish tribes were the Salians and the Riparians, who settled in what is now Belgium. And it was the Salian Franks which at length became the dominant tribe. Their first king of any account was Clovis. He traced his descent from a mythical sea-king called Merovée, and from that the dynasty to which he belonged is called the Merovingian dynasty.

Clovis came to the throne at the age of sixteen. He soon set out upon a career of conquest, and in no long time doubled and trebled his kingdom.

At the time of their invasion of the Empire nearly all the Teutonic tribes were Christian. But they were Arian Christians—that is, they were followers of Arius, whose doctrine, to put it simply, was a sort of early Unitarianism. It was easier for the uneducated Teutons to understand this doctrine than the more complicated one of the Trinity, and therefore they adopted it.

Arianism

Arianism has long since passed away, and it may not seem to matter very much what those half-civilized tribes believed. But in the reconstruction of Europe after the fall of the Roman Empire it had some importance. For the fact that the Teutons were Arians made for them an enemy in the Bishop of Rome, who was gradually becoming a power in temporal as well as in spiritual matters.

But although most of the barbarians who attacked the Empire were Christian, some were not. Among those who were not were the Angles and the Saxons, who took possession of England, and the Franks.

Clovis, like the people over whom he ruled, was a heathen, but he married a Christian princess, Clotilda, the niece of the King of Burgundy. And this Clotilda was not an Arian like her uncle, but a Catholic. She was very devout, and she tried very earnestly to convert her heathen husband. But Clovis resisted all her efforts. He allowed her undisturbed to follow her own religion, but he was satisfied with his own gods, and refused to change. At last, however, Clotilda had her wish.

Clovis was fighting against the Allemanni, and in the Battle of Tolbiac his soldiers were being beaten. Fervently he called upon his heathen gods to save him, and turn the fortune of the day in his favour. His prayers were in vain, and the Franks fled before the foe. Then, in the agony of defeat, Clovis prayed to Clotilda's God.
"Jesus Christ," he cried, "whom Clotilda declares to be the only true God, aid me. If Thou wilt grant me victory over mine enemies I will believe in Thee, and will be baptized in Thy name. I have called upon my own gods and they have not helped me. To Thee alone I pray."

As Clovis so prayed the tide of battle turned, and when night fell the victory was his, and the enemy fled in all directions. Returning home, the king loyally kept his word. The water of baptism was sprinkled upon him, his forehead received the sign of the Cross, and henceforth he was a Christian. Nor was Clovis alone in his baptism. With him three hundred of his followers accepted the Christian faith.

This sudden and wholesale conversion made little difference in the lives of Clovis and his tameless warriors. After, as before, they were blood-thirsty barbarians. But much of the king's future success was due to his conversion. For it brought him a powerful friend in the Church of Rome, and when he conquered the Arian kings of the Visigoths and the Burgundians, the great prelates looked upon him as a champion of the

Church, and regarded his wars as holy wars. Thus began an alliance between the popes and the kings of France which, in days to come, had great influence upon the history of western Europe.

Even the emperor in far-off Constantinople honoured Clovis. Instead of regarding him as a barbarian enemy, assisting at the destruction of the Empire, he looked upon him as an ally, and gave him the title of Roman Consul. It was but an empty title, and added nothing to the reality of the Frankish king's conquests, but it pleased his barbaric mind.

Clovis reigned for thirty years. At the beginning of his reign he had been merely the chief of a petty tribe. When he died he was ruler of a vast kingdom stretching from beyond the Rhine to the Pyrenees. "For each day," says an old writer, "the enemies of Clovis fell beneath his hand, and his kingdom was augmented, because with a pure heart he walked before the Lord, and did that which was right in His eyes."

THE BARBARIANS RULE IN ROME

ROME had been saved from the Hun (see Chapter I) only to fall into the hands of another barbarian foe. From Andalusia the Vandals had crossed the Straits of Gibraltar, overrun the northern shores of Africa, and, under their savage king, Gaiseric, made themselves complete masters of that Roman province. Up and down the Mediterranean they sailed in their pirate ships, plundering the rich and fruitful islands, causing peaceful traders to tremble and flee before them. Their sole joy was in plunder and bloodshed, and they cared not where they went in quest of it.

The Vandals: The March of Gaiseric

"I sail to the cities of men with whom God is angry," said Gaiseric. And from his actions it would appear that he thought God was angry with all who crossed his path. So, having robbed and wasted many a fair city of the Mediterranean, Gaiseric and his Vandals one day appeared before Rome. The emperor and the people fled, and the walls were left defenceless. But as the Vandals advanced the gates were thrown open. It was, however, no armed force which issued forth, but a company of priests.

Once again Leo sought to save the imperial city. Unarmed save by his dauntless courage, with the Cross carried before him, and his clergy following after, he advanced to meet the foe. But this time he could not altogether prevail. The Vandals were bent on booty. Booty they would have. Leo could only wring from their chief a promise that there should be no bloodshed, no burning of houses, no torture of the defenceless. With that he was fain to be content, and the sack of Rome began.

For fourteen days the pillage lasted. Then, having stripped the city of its treasures, the robbers sailed away in their richly laden galleys, carrying with them thousands of Roman citizens as slaves.

The Western Empire was now almost entirely in the hands of the Teutonic tribes which had overrun its borders. But still, for twenty-one years, it lingered on in death. Then the end came.

The last emperor of Rome bore the same name as its founder—

Romulus. He was, however, only a feeble, beautiful boy of fourteen, so he was called Romulus Augustulus or the Little Emperor. He was deposed by Odoacer the German, who was the first barbarian to sit upon the throne of the Cæsars. Odoacer, however, did not take to himself the title of emperor. For the Roman Empire in the east still existed, a Roman emperor still reigned in Constantinople. To this emperor then, Odoacer sent the purple robe and the royal diadem, with a letter, in which he declared that one emperor was enough both for East and West, and demanding the right to rule in Italy as patrician or king.

Theodoric and the Ostrogoths

At first, when the emperor, Zeno, received Odoacer's letter he was merely angry that this bold barbarian had dared to usurp the throne of the Cæsars. Then he felt rather pleased at the idea of being sole emperor. So he left Odoacer alone, and for thirteen years he reaped the reward of his boldness, and ruled Rome in peace. Then another barbarian, Theodoric the Ostrogoth, turned his eyes on Italy. He desired to conquer it, and the emperor did nothing to restrain him. For Theodoric and his Goths were dangerous friends and troublesome neighbours, and it seemed better to the emperor that they should harass the Western Empire, over which he had but a shadowy right, than that they should turn their swords against him.

So once again a great barbarian force marched on Italy. This time they came not as an army but as a nation, bringing their wives, and children and household goods with them. For the Goths had heard much of the beauty and the riches of Rome, and they meant to abide there. Odoacer, however, did not lightly yield what his sword had won, and for more than four years he fought for his kingdom. At length, however, even his stubborn will gave way, and at Ravenna he surrendered to Theodoric.

Theodoric promised Odoacer his life, promised even that he should rule with equal power with himself. But he did not keep his promise, for he well knew that two kings could not rule in Italy, and secretly he resolved to put Odoacer to death.

Ten days, therefore, after Theodoric had entered Ravenna in triumph he invited his fallen rival to a feast. As Odoacer neared the banqueting hall two men suddenly threw themselves at his feet, praying him to grant them a boon. In the fervour of their entreaties they seized his hands and held them fast. As they did so armed men, in the midst of whom was Theodoric, drawn sword in hand, surrounded them. Too well Odoacer knew that his last hour had come. "O God," he cried, "where art Thou?"

He spoke no more. For Theodoric's sword descended, cleaving his helpless enemy from neck to thigh. Even Theodoric himself was amazed at the blow. "Methinks the catiff had never a bone in his body!" he cried, with a savage laugh, as he turned away.

Thus Theodoric the Goth began his reign in Italy, and save this one black deed of treachery there is little to record against him in his reign of more than thirty years. He was a barbarian, but with the conquest of Italy he stayed his sword, seeking no further conquests, but only the good of the conquered people.

He had no easy task, for he had two utterly different peoples to rule over, Romans and Goths. He was just, however, and wise, and soon he was loved by both peoples. He preserved many of the old Roman laws, and although he was so ignorant himself that he could only with difficulty trace his own name, he encouraged learning in others. He made friendly alliances with all the peoples around him, and so that these should be lasting and binding he arranged marriages between his own family and those of the neighbouring princes, thus taking a precaution of which the world has not yet learned the uselessness and danger.

Theodoric, indeed, seems to have been for these early days a model prince. He was, we are told, "A lover of manufactures, and a great restorer of cities. . . . Merchants from other countries flocked to his dominions. For so great was the order which he made there that if any one left gold or silver at his farm it was as safe as if it had been within a walled city. This is proved by the fact that he never made gates for any city in Italy, and those which were there already were never closed."

It seemed as if Theodoric had founded a new dynasty in Italy, under which those two races, from which the modern civilization of Europe was to spring, would be united. But that was not to be. After a reign of nearly thirty-three years he died, leaving his kingdom to the rule of a woman and a child, and all the miseries attendant.

THE RISE AND FALL OF JUSTINIAN'S EMPIRE— THE ROLE OF THE EASTERN EMPIRE

THE year after Theodoric died Justinian, one of the greatest rulers of the Eastern Empire, came to power. He was not content with merely ruling over the Eastern Empire, but, like the Cæsars before him, he had dreams of a world dominion, and he longed to gather under his sceptre all the lands which had at one time owned Roman sway. He had great generals at his command to help him to realize his dream, among them Belisarius, at this time a brave and splendid youth.

Belisarius and Narses

About this time the Vandals were quarrelling among themselves, and it seemed to Justinian a good opportunity to win Africa again for the Empire. So with a great army Belisarius set out. In a campaign of three months he conquered the Vandals. Then, laden with rich spoil, and carrying the captive Vandal king, Gelimer, with him, he returned again to Constantinople in triumph.

Italy, too, was at this time in a state of unrest. Here again Justinian saw his opportunity, and again Belisarius set forth to subdue a rebel province of the Empire. But to conquer the Goths was by no means an easy matter. The war raged for years, and before he could bring it to a victorious close the jealousy of his rivals caused Belisarius to be recalled.

Two years later he returned to Italy. But he was, he says himself, "destitute of all the necessary implements of war—men, horses, arms, and money." And the emperor, still listening to the envious whisperers, was deaf to his appeals. So the war lingered on, until at length Belisarius was again recalled, and his place taken by Narses, another of Justinian's great generals.

Narses was no young and splendid hero like Belisarius, but a little dried-up old man. He was, however, the most brilliant strategist of the day, and he received the support denied to Belisarius. His so-called Roman army was indeed merely a conglomeration of Greeks and wild barbarians, but with it he swept victoriously through Italy.

It was not far from the ancient city of Pompeii that the Goths made their last stand. Their king, Teias, stood in the forefront of the battle. In his right hand he held a mighty spear, and with unerring aim he dealt death this way and that. Although arrows and javelins fell thick and fast about him, he heeded them not. Yet so many found their mark, and remained fast embedded in his shield that, at length, even his mighty arm could not bear the weight.

So calling to his squire he bade him bring another shield. The squire obeyed. But for one moment, in changing one shield for another, the king's side was unprotected. In that moment a javelin was sped, and, pierced to the heart, Teias fell dying to the ground. With a wild shout of exultation the foe rushed forward, and cutting off his head, placed it upon a spear, and carried it in triumph through their ranks.

Thus died the last king of the Goths. Yet although leaderless now, his men still fought on, and only night and darkness put an end to the strife. Day dawned and it was renewed, but the struggle now was hopeless, and at length the Goths sued for peace. This Narses readily granted, giving the conquered people the choice between remaining in Italy as the subjects of Justinian or of departing thence.

The Goths chose to depart. And with their women and children and household goods they slowly crossed the Alps. They went who knows where? From that time the Ostrogoths vanish from history.

But the campaign in Italy was not yet over. For the Franks and Allemanni had poured like a torrent over the Alps into the plain of Italy, vowing to restore the Gothic kingdom. But these, too, Narses defeated, and only a scattered remnant reached home. Then at length the harassed, exhausted land had rest, and for the next twelve years Narses ruled over it as governor for the emperor.

Justinian also attacked the Visigoths in Spain, and brought all the south and east of that country under Roman rule once more. So much of the old Roman Empire, indeed, did he reconquer that it seemed as if his dream might come true. But in 565 he died, and almost at once fresh hordes of barbarians overran his newly acquired provinces. The Lombards invaded Italy, the Visigoths rose and expelled the Romans from Spain, Slavs and Avars, wild peoples akin to the Huns, streamed over the Balkans, while Persians, in a war which lasted twenty years, devasted the eastern boundaries of the Empire. Arabs made themselves masters of Egypt and

Roman Africa, until at length the Eastern Empire included little more than the countries now forming Greece, the Balkan States, and Asia Minor.

It is not, therefore, for his conquests that we remember Justinian. For his conquests soon vanished away, and all through the ages he has been remembered not as a conqueror but as a lawgiver. His great work was the codification of the whole body of Roman law. Upon the so-called laws of Justinian the laws of nearly every civilized country are founded to this day. That is his title to greatness.

It must be remembered, too, that although after the time of Justinian the dimensions of the Empire became small indeed, in comparison to those of the Roman Empire in the days of its strength, it was no mean role that this shrunken Empire played in the development of Europe; for it formed a Christian bulwark against the attacks of the heathen hordes of Asia. While the new Teutonic kingdoms were being formed it was the Romans and not the Teutons who defended Europe from the danger coming from the east.

And besides being a barrier the Eastern Empire was a storehouse of art and literature. For the new Teutonic nations which overran the Western Empire were only half civilized, or not civilized at all. Before them the learning and the art of old Rome went down. It would have been lost to the world had it not been kept alive in Constantinople. There, too, in this time of flux the trade and commerce of Europe centred, and when in course of time the new Teutonic kingdoms settled down, and the peoples awakened to the need of learning and of art, it was to Constantinople that they turned to find them.

But however useful a part the Empire played in the development of Europe the old imperial splendour was gone. New Rome was not mistress of the world, but rather its handmaid. And as the old imperial idea changed the character of the Empire changed too. It was no longer Roman in any sense, but Greek. Greek became the language of State, and even the later laws of Justinian were written in that language. So although legally the continuance of the Roman Empire, it has come to be called the Greek Empire or the Byzantine Empire, from the name of the ancient city of Byzantium, upon the site of which Constantinople was built.

GREGORY THE GREAT LAYS THE
FOUNDATION OF PAPAL POWER

Lombards in Italy

THE Lombards or Longbeards, so called either because of their long axes or long beards, invaded Italy less than three years after the death of Justinian. They were a terrible people, "a race fierce with more than the ordinary fierceness of the Germans." They fought for the mere love of bloodshed and destruction. They had not even the beginnings of art and learning when they swarmed over Italy, and they brought nothing with them save savagery and a cruel love of slaughter.

The name of their king at this time was Albion, and with his brutish host he quickly overran all the north of the peninsula, made Pavia his capital, and called himself Lord of Italy. In no long time, however, Albion was murdered by his own people. His successor also was murdered. Then for ten years there followed a "kingless time," during which thirty-six barbarian dukes oppressed the unhappy land.

Soon the whole peninsula was theirs save Ravenna, Rome, Naples, Venice, and a few other coast towns with the territory round them. All Italy was still in name part of the Eastern Empire, and an exarch ruled in Ravenna in the name of the emperor. But he could give little help to the rest of Italy against the Lombards, for he had scarce troops enough to defend Ravenna itself.

Now again and again in their misery the Romans sent messengers to Constantinople, praying the emperors who succeeded Justinian to grant them aid. But they prayed in vain. The emperors were busy with their wars against the Persians and the Avars, enemies at their gates. To them Constantinople was the heart of the Empire, Italy but an outlying province, for which it was not well to sacrifice safety at home.

Such was the state of Italy when, in 590, much against his will, Gregory I became pope. "For my sins," he writes, "I find myself bishop, not of the Romans but of the Lombards, men whose promises stab like swords, and whose kindness is bitter punishment."

In his youth Gregory had been a brilliant man of the world, and had been made prefect of the city, an office which entitled him to wear the imperial purple. We may picture him, young and handsome, dashing through the streets of Rome in a gilded chariot, while the populace bow before him, or clad in robes of purple presiding at the Senate, or in the courts of justice. But amidst this splendour Gregory felt the call of religion. Suddenly he broke off his brilliant career, devoted all his fortune to the founding of convents and monasteries, and himself became a monk.

But Gregory had a true genius for business, and his great abilities could not be altogether hid beneath the humble garb of a monk. He soon became an abbot, and at length the supreme office of pope was thrust upon him. As pope he showed himself to be a great pastor and great statesman. His love for, and pride in, Rome was unbounded. To him there was no question but that Rome was the city of the world, and that the bishop of Rome was by divine right the head of the Church. And by insisting on that right he laid the foundations of the absolute spiritual power which future popes were to enjoy.

The Temporal Power of the Papacy

He also laid the foundations of their temporal power. This was not so much sought by him as forced upon him by cir-cumstances. His appeals for help against the Lombards were disregarded both by the exarch of Ravenna and by the emperor. He saw then that he must either take to himself regal power or suffer the oppression of the Lombards. He chose the former, and boldly took the reins of government into his own hands. He carried on the war against the Lombards, he gave orders to generals, he appointed governors, and did not hesitate to declare that his rank was higher than that of the exarch, even although the latter was the representative of the emperor. Finally he made peace on his own account with one of the Lombard chiefs.

This roused the Emperor Maurice to wrath, and he called Gregory in so many words a disloyal, presumptuous fool. He could, or would, do nothing himself to relieve his distressed province, but neither would he recognize the act of another which seemed to usurp his imperial authority, and he refused to ratify the peace. Only after years had passed could he be brought to own that the Lombards had come to stay, and see the impossibility of ousting them without strong measures. For strong measures he was not prepared, and at length a general peace was signed.

16

Peace brought added work to Gregory both in Church and State. For now that his messengers could travel safely through Italy he made rebellious or lax clergy feel his authority, rousing them to zeal or bringing them back to obedience. He settled disputes over boundaries, and arbitrated in many ways between Lombards and Romans. Now, too, he carried out his long cherished plan and sent St. Augustine to convert the heathen Angles of England.

Gregory's days and nights were full, his manifold labours leaving him scant rest. Yet all this work in Church and state, at home and abroad, was carried on by a man in constant pain, so ill indeed that for weeks at a time he could not leave his bed. "I live in such misery and pain," he writes, "that I grieve to see the light of returning day. My only comfort is in the hope of death." Or again, "I die daily, yet never die."

Before many years had passed his labours for peace seemed to be brought to naught by the folly of the exarch. War broke out again and ended in further triumphs for the Lombards. Yet from this time dates a more settled state in the affairs of Italy. The peace was often disturbed, often broken, but on the whole it was maintained, or renewed, from year to year. Still, for nearly two hundred years this obscure and savage Teuton race held sway over the fair lands of Italy which to-day still bear the name of Lombardy.

Meanwhile the great prelate drew near his end. A moment of peace had come to his beloved land when peace came to him too, and death set him free from his labours and his pains. He was not as men count years an aged man, but he was worn out by his great labours and great suffering. He left his mark not only on his own times but on times to come. For he had advanced the Roman see to a far higher position than it had ever before attained, and for good or ill had laid the foundations of the temporal power of the popes.

THE RISE OF MOHAMMEDANISM

ABOUT four or five years after the death of Justinian the Great a little boy was born in Mecca, and was given the name of Mohammed, or the Praised. This Arab belonged to a princely tribe who traced their descent to Ishmael. They had in their keeping the Kaabah or sacred temple of the Arabs. Kaabah means a cube, and the name was given to the temple because of its shape, which was square. It had only one window and one door, and until the time of Mohammed it was roofed only by a great black carpet which hung down on all sides.

This temple was said to have been first built by Adam from a plan sent down from heaven. But it had been restored several times, by Seth, by Abraham, and last by Ishmael. Since that time the tribe to which Mohammed belonged had had it in their keeping. It enshrined a great treasure, for in the north-west corner of the wall there was set a black stone which was said to have been brought from paradise. Then it was white, but it had since turned black through the many kisses bestowed upon it by sinful although devout lips.

In spite of this legend, which seems to connect them with the Jews, the Arabs were idolaters, and within the Kaabah there were gathered three hundred and sixty idols in the shapes of men and beasts. Every year vast numbers of pilgrims came from all parts of Arabia to do homage to them and, above all, to the sacred black stone. The possession of this stone made the Kaabah the most venerated temple in all Arabia, indeed, because of it the whole district round Mecca was considered holy, and it was forbidden to kill anything there save animals for sacrifice.

It was therefore in a city already held sacred that Mohammed was born. He caused it to be held still more sacred, and made the name of Mecca famous throughout the whole world.

Mohammed's father died before he was born, and his mother and grandfather not many years later. He had many uncles, and as they claimed much of his father's fortune there was little left for Mohammed. So he began life with no more wealth than five camels and a slave girl. But he was fortunate and prospered well. He was a splendid-looking man, broad

18

of shoulder, lithe of limb, with great black eyes shining in his clear brown face. He seemed born to lead and bend others to his will. Yet he was forty years old before he began the career which made him famous.

At this time many people in Arabia were dissatisfied with the worship of idols, and were seeking after a better religion. Some of Mohammed's friends were among these. He used to talk much with them, and also with the many Jews and Christians who had settled in the land, and from them he learned something both of the Jewish and of the Christian faiths.

Mohammed pondered over these things, and at length he announced that he had seen a vision, and received a revelation from heaven. One day, he said, when he was in a lonely spot an angel appeared to him with a written scroll in his hand, and said to him, "Read."

Now Mohammed could neither read nor write, and in great fear he replied, "I cannot read." Thereupon the angel shook him wrathfully, and again commanded him to read. Again Mohammed, in great fear and trembling, replied, "I cannot read."

Three times this was repeated. Then the angel himself took the scroll and read it to Mohammed, and the words which he heard were so graven upon his heart that he remembered them ever after, and later, when his holy book was made, they became part of it.

Other visions and revelations followed this first one, and at length Mohammed announced his message to the world. It was very simple. It was merely, "There is but one God and Mohammed is his prophet."

Thus a new religion was founded which was, in time, to enslave half the world. But at first few listened to Mohammed. Indeed, for some years he made scarcely any converts save the women of his own household. But by degrees, slowly at first, and then more rapidly, his followers increased.

And as Mohammed's followers increased, visions and revelations increased also. For when anything required to be added to the creed, or when any action of the Prophet seemed to need supernatural support, Mohammed had a revelation. What he learned in these Mohammed dictated to his scribes, who wrote it down on palm leaves, blade bones of animals, bits of parchment, or anything which came to hand. It was not

19

until after the Prophet's death, however, that they were all gathered together into the Koran, or Book of God of the Mohammedans.

The Hegira

In time Mohammed had adherents all over Arabia. Only the men of his own tribe were filled with wrath against him. For, said they, if this pestilent fellow preached that there was only one God what was to become of the Kaabah and its many idols. If the idols fell into disrepute the keepers of the temple would be ruined. The thousands of pilgrims who flocked every year to the Kaabah would come no more. All the trade which came in their train, which made not only the keepers of the temple but Mecca rich and powerful, would be lost. They decided, therefore, that his mouth must be stopped, and a persecution began which ended in Mohammed fleeing with his followers to Medina. This is called the Hegira, or Flight, and from it the beginning of the Mohammedan era dates.

It was soon after the Hegira that Mohammed began to preach his holy war. He had taken a great deal of his new religion from Judaism and from Christianity. But unlike these religions, which either did not try to make converts, or tried to make them peacefully, Mohammed now determined to convert the world with the sword if need be.

So Mohammed unsheathed his sword, and in less than eight years' time he who had fled from Mecca in secrecy and darkness returned in triumph. He entered the Kaabah, and ordered it to be cleared of idols. And as one by one they fell beneath the blows of his followers, he cried in exultation, "Truth hath come. Falsehood hath gone; for falsehood vanisheth away."

But although cleared of idols the Kaabah still remained the holy of holies to the followers of Mohammed, and Mecca is still the holy city towards which every Mohammedan turns when he prays. For Mohammed quickly saw that unless he preserved the sacred character of Mecca he could never win his fellow-countrymen to his creed. During countless ages they had worshipped at Mecca, and reverence for it was bred in them. So Mohammed kept Mecca as his holy city. And when the Arabs found that they might confess the new creed, and still worship in the Kaabah, thousands became easy converts.

Thus he who had begun life with no fortune save five camels and a

20

slave girl made himself master of an empire. Mohammed found Arabia a mass of hostile tribes, each with its own laws, and perpetually at war with every other tribe round. He found it given over to idolatry. In twenty years he united the warring tribes and made them monotheistic. In twenty years he created a nation with a national religion and national laws.

But Mohammed's ambition was not bounded by Arabia. He determined to force his religion on people beyond its borders and, even before Mecca had submitted to him, he had caused letters to be written to the greatest potentates of the world, to the Byzantine emperor, to the king of Persia, and to the rulers of many lesser states. These letters he sealed with a great seal, engraven with the words, "Mohammed, the Apostle of God." In haughty words he bade these proud potentates put away their old idolatrous religions, and do homage to the one true God.

But as yet the name of Mohammed was hardly known beyond the borders of Arabia, and his haughty missives awoke no thrill of fear in the breasts of the august princes to whom they were addressed. Some of the lesser rulers answered courteously enough, but the greatest among them, the Emperor Heraclius, flung the letter contemptuously by, while Chosroes, the king of Persia, tore his to atoms in fury, and commanded that the insolent Arab be brought to him in chains. When Mohammed heard what reception his letter had received he, too, was wrathful. He cursed the arrogant king. "Even as he has rent Thy message, O Lord," he cried, "wilt Thou rend his kingdom from him."

Indeed, the time was not far distant when both king and emperor were to tremble at the name of the upstart Arab. But Mohammed himself did not live to see that time, for two years after his triumphant return to Mecca he died. It seemed for a time as if his work had died with him. But it was not so, for he had breathed the spirit of his enthusiasm into others, and he was succeeded by his faithful friend and father-in-law Abu Bekr. He was the first caliph, caliph meaning merely successor.

THE CONQUEST OF SPAIN
BY THE ARABS

The Conquests of Abu Bekr

ABU BEKR was filled with as great a zeal for the faith as had been Mohammed, and with an even greater lust for gold and power. So the triumphant march of the Moslems, or Saracens as they came to be called, through the world began. With sword in one hand and Book of God in the other they set out to conquer and convert the whole world. To all prisoners of war they offered but one choice—death or the Koran.

Thus a new terror was born into the world, a new danger made all Europe tremble, and for many ages the cry of Allah, Allah! was to blanche the cheek and wake fear in the hearts of all who heard it.

The Moslem soldiers were as fearless as they were feared. Death to them had no terrors. It was but the gateway into a new and glorious life; for they believed that if they died fighting for their faith they would at once enter into a paradise of endless delights. If they hesitated, only the pains of hell awaited them.

So with fanatic zeal and lust of blood and of gold burning in them, the dark-faced horde swept onward. All Persia fell before them, from the Caspian Sea to the Indus. Syria the Holy Land, Armenia, were torn from the Empire. Egypt, too, bowed to the yoke. Yet Constantinople stood firm, and again and yet again the ravening host was rolled back from its walls discomfited.

But through the Golden Gate of Constantinople was not the only way of reaching Europe. The Mediterranean lay open to the Moslem ships, and soon the trade routes of the world were in their hands. Throughout the length and breadth of the inland sea they sailed at will. They overran the north of Africa, and the kingdom of the Vandals, which Justinian had reconquered for the Eastern Empire, became another jewel in the caliph's crown. Through Africa the conquering Arab marched until he reached the shores of the Atlantic. There, like some new Alexander, he stood, sighing for more worlds to conquer. Westward lay the barren Outer Sea, the great double continent which lay across its wide waters still unknown and unguessed at. Southward lay the trackless desert. Northward then to Europe the conqueror's eyes were turned.

Across the narrrow Straits lay Spain. Since the days when Ataulphus the son of the Wolf had led his followers there (see Chapter I) the power of the Visigoths had spread until at length they held sway over the whole of what is now Spain, and over a great part of southern Gaul as well. For nearly three centuries foreign foes had scarcely touched their borders. Yet the Goths did not prosper. For they were a turbulent people, and the kingdom was nearly always in a state of unrest. Many of their kings died by murder, many were deposed, revolutions were frequent and bloody.

Roderick and Tarick

Now, instead of uniting against the Moslem danger, they still quarrelled among themselves. A noble named Roderick had usurped the throne. But there were many who hated him, among them the sons of the late king, and a certain Julian, to whom he had done a deadly wrong. The Jews, too, of whom there were many in the land, were ready to revolt, for they were cruelly persecuted.

The Arab love of plunder was well known, and it seemed to all these malcontents that it would be well to have their help to depose the hated king, Roderick. The Arabs would come, thought the Visigoths, defeat and depose their king, and, having plundered him to their heart's content, would depart again to their own land.

So Count Julian went to the Arab leader and offered to help him if he would but come and free the country from the yoke of the usurper. The Moslems were willing enough, and a young and skilful officer named Tarick was sent to depose King Roderick. He landed at the rocky south-western corner of Europe which, after him, was called Jebal-Tarick, or the rock of Tarick. It is still called by that name, Gibraltar, although the last syllable has fallen away.

Upon landing, Tarick fortified his camp, and thus more than twelve hundred years ago began the military history of one of the most famous fortresses of the world. King Roderick hastened to meet Tarick, and not far from the town of Xeres a great fight took place But when the armies drew near to each other, we are told, "the Gothic princes began to spin the web of treason." They, with their followers, deserted and joined the Saracen ranks, and soon the rest of the Gothic army broke and fled in disorder.

King Roderick had entered the battle as if he were going to a play, so disdainful was he of the heathen invader. Clad in flowing silken robes, with a jewelled diadem about his brow, he reclined in an ivory car, drawn by milk-white mules. But when he saw the day lost and his soldiers fleeing in rout, he sprang from the car, and leaping upon his fleetest horse, joined the rout. He fled from battle, however, only to meet death in another fashion. For in trying to cross a river, which flowed near the battlefield, he was drowned.

The Saracen victory was complete. But instead of being content with their triumph and plunder, as Count Julian and his fellow-conspirators had imagined, the victorious troops marched further and further into Spain. Everywhere towns opened their gates to them. Hardly anywhere did they meet with the slightest resistance, and in a few months the Visigothic kingdom was wiped from the map of Europe. It vanished even as the Ostrogothic kingdom had vanished, and the whole of Spain, save a little strip in the north-west, became a province of the great Mohammedan Empire.

But the conquerors were not content with Spain only. They swept on over the Pyrenees, and before long all the south of Gaul was in their hands. Nothing, it seemed, could stay their conquering march. In less than a century and a half the Arabs had built up almost the greatest empire the world has ever seen. Now it appeared as if all Europe might bow the knee to Allah, and pay tribute to the caliph.

Arab Rule in Spain

Yet it is well to remember that where the conquering Arab passed he did not destroy as the Hun and the Goth destroyed. Beneath the onslaught of the Christian, but more than half barbaric Teutons, the art and learning of Rome to a great extent disappeared, and Italy especially was left forlorn and desolate.

It was not so much that the Teutons deliberately set themselves to destroy the splendid monuments of Roman art and learning, as we are taught to imagine by the modern use of Goth and Vandal. Indeed, many of the chief Teutonic leaders had been trained in the school of Rome, and desired to preserve all that was best of Roman tradition. But even so, the genius of the two peoples was so diverse that much that was Roman was bound to disappear. Besides, although some of the leaders were more or less civilized, their followers were still brutishly ignorant.

War was the only art known to the mass of the Teutons when they invaded the Empire. For a long time after their invasion war was the rule rather than the exception, and people who live in a constant state of war cannot well cultivate the arts of peace.

With the Arabs it was different. At the time of their irruption into Europe they were already advanced in arts and learning. They brought their learning with them and implanted it in the conquered countries. And for many generations Spain owed her advance in the arts of peace to the domination of the Arabs.

THE DEFEAT OF THE SARACENS—
THE RISE OF THE CAROLINGIANS—
THE DONATION OF PEPIN

IN the east Christian Constantinople had stood as a bulwark against the Arab invasion. But in spite of that the Mohammedans had made an entrance through the western gate of Europe, and it seemed as if nothing could now stay their conquering march. Yet stayed it was.

The kingdom of the Franks (see Chapter II) was the only one of the Teutonic kingdoms built upon the ruins of the Roman Empire which was to endure. But for many years after the reign of Clovis its history was one of turmoil and bloodshed. It was divided and redivided more than once. After a time the Merovingian kings lost their vigour and manliness. They became mere figureheads and are known as the Rois Fainéants or Do Nothing kings.

Surrounded by luxury and pomp, they sat in their palaces, combing their long golden hair, indolently dreaming the time away, while all the business of state drifted more and more into the hands of the mayors of the palace. These mayors had been at first little more than the managers of the royal household; in time they became dukes, and at length kings in all but name.

Charles the Hammer

The greatest of the mayors was Charles the Hammer. It was he who now gathered all the strength of the Frankish kingdom to fight the Saracen foe, and roll back the dark menace of Mohammedanism from western Europe.

The battle in which the Franks and Saracens met is one of the memorable battles of the world. For it was not so much the Franks and Saracens who were arrayed against each other as Europe and Asia, Christianity and Mohammedanism. If the Franks were beaten, then all Europe was at the mercy of the Saracens. For behind the Franks there was no power to stop their march, nothing but still heathen Germany. It was true Constantinople held the gate of Europe in the east. But if the foe made an entry in the west would that shut gate avail?

Battle of Tours

The fight which now took place between these two great forces is often called the battle of Tours, but it was really fought nearer the town of Poitiers. Here the fair Teutons of the north, steel clad, heavily armed, and somewhat slow of movement, met the dark-faced, agile men of Asia. Mounted upon Arab coursers, the Saracens again and again dashed upon the solid wall of the Teutons. Again and again they were broken and scattered like waves upon a rocky coast. Yet, undismayed, they returned to the attack, and above the din of clashing steel there rose the shout, "Allah, Allah Akbar!"

The fortune of the day seemed uncertain. Then suddenly throughout the Saracen army the cry arose that the Christians were attacking from behind, and that the Saracen camp with all its rich booty was in danger. In a flash a great body of the Arab cavalry wheeled about, and dashed to save the treasure. Their greed cost them the day. With a shout the Franks charged, and before that mighty onslaught the Arabs fled like dust before the wind.

The sun went down upon the victory of the Franks. But how complete that victory was Charles the Hammer did not know until next morning, when he found the Arab camp empty and deserted. Nor did he at this time follow up his advantage. Seven years later, however, he again attacked the Saracens, and at length drove them out of France altogether. Hence his name—the Hammer.

By his victories over the Saracens Charles made a great name for himself, and the pope, now Gregory III, sent to him to implore aid against the Lombards, who still distressed Italy. But Charles was friendly with the Lombard king, Luitprand, and had no wish to fight against him. So, although he received the pope's messenger with all honour, and loaded him with gifts, he sent him back to Rome without any promise of help. Again the following year Gregory sent to Charles, abjuring him by the true and living God not to prefer the friendship of the Lombards to that of the prince of the Apostles. But again Charles failed to give the answer for which the pope craved, and soon afterwards he died.

27

Pepin and the Pope

Charles had been king of the Franks in all but name, and now his son Pepin, who ruled after him, made up his mind to be king in name as well as in fact. So he sent messengers to the pope, now Zacharias, to ask whether he who remained in his palace free from all peril, or he who had the cares and dangers of the kingdom on his shoulders, should have the title of king.

Already it would seem as if the pope was regarded as a lawgiver to princes, and Zacharias replied as Pepin had desired he should. "By the authority of the Apostle Peter" he bade the Franks acknowledge for their king he who possessed the royal power. So the last Merovingian king was shorn of his flowing locks, the sign of his sovereignty, and sent to end his days in a convent, and Pepin became the first Carolingian king of the Franks.

The accession of Pepin was not merely the beginning of a new dynasty. It was the beginning of new claims both for king and priest, it was an exalting both of Church and state. Formerly when the Franks had chosen a chief, standing upon his shield he was raised shoulder high by his warriors, who acclaimed him king and ruler. Now with solemn ceremony, surrounded by bishops and priests, Pepin was led to the great church at Soissons. There, kneeling upon the steps of the altar, he was crowned and anointed by Boniface, the Apostle of the Germans. He was the chosen now of God and of the Church, and kingship took a new and holy character.

Pepin, King by the Grace of God

Here we have the beginning of "kings by the Grace of God," and of that "divine right" which in days to come was to bring in its train such grievous woes and cause such desperate struggles between kings and peoples.

The pope already looked upon Pepin's crown as the gift of the Church. And the gifts of the Church were not given without expectation of return. So very soon Pepin was called upon to show his gratitude. For the year after his coronation a new Lombard king and a new pope ruled in Italy, and, disregarding the peace which had been made by King Luitprand, King Aistulph renewed the attacks on Rome and on Ravenna. The pope,

Stephen II, then sent piteous appeals for help to Pepin, and as he did not yield to them immediately, he resolved to make an appeal in person.

Midwinter although it was, he hastened across the Alps, braving "frost and snow, many waters and rushing torrents," as he himself writes. But in spite of hardships and dangers he reached France in safety, and followed by his priests he went at once to greet the king. Clad in a coarse woollen robe, and with ashes sprinkled on his head, he bowed himself before Pepin, imploring his help. Nor would he rise until his prayer was granted.

Pepin promised the aid for which the pope begged, and in return the pope once more crowned Pepin, and anointed both his queen and her children. Then, under pain of excommunication, he forbade the Franks ever to choose a king save from this family "thus consecrated upon the intercession of the holy Apostles by the hands of their vicar the sovereign pontiff."

The new coronation over, the pope gave to Pepin and his sons the title of patrician of Rome. It was a title created by Constantine the Great, and could be conferred only by an emperor, so in giving it to Pepin and his sons Stephen usurped the authority of the emperor. But as the emperor showed himself more and more incapable of protecting Rome, and more and more indifferent to its fate, both pope and people had begun to forget that they owed any allegiance to him, and this usurpation was only one among many signs that Italy was no longer truly a part of the Empire.

Shortly after his second coronation Pepin set out to redeem his promise to Stephen. In two campaigns he conquered the Lombards king, Aistulph, and forced him to give up Ravenna and the other parts of Italy which he had lately seized.

The Donation of Pepin

Italy, and especially Ravenna, were still in theory part of the Empire. But Pepin considered that these provinces were now his by right of conquest, and that he could do with them as he pleased. And so much of a phantom had the right of the emperor become that he caused a deed of gift to be written out, bestowing the conquered lands not upon the emperor but upon St. Peter and his successors, the sovereign pontiffs, for all time.

The pope well knew the value of the gift. With solemn ceremony the keys of the conquered cities, together with the deed of gift, were laid upon the tomb of St. Peter in Rome. Then they were locked up by the pope among his most precious treasures.

This presentation of lands to the pope is called the Donation of Pepin. By it the Papal States were founded, and the pope, from being little more than a priestly farmer, became a ruling prince, and took his place among the sovereigns of Europe. Thus king and pope helped to make each other great. But there seems little question that the pope was the greater gainer. The king had only received the Church's sanction to hold the kingdom which he, in fact, already had; the pope had gained possession of a kingdom which without Pepin's aid he could never have hoped to win. Yet in the long run by thus entering the ranks of temporal rulers the Church was to lose as a spiritual institution and power for good.

THE REIGN OF CHARLEMAGNE—THE BEGINNING
OF THE HOLY ROMAN EMPIRE

IN A.D. 768 Charles the Great, or Charlemagne as he is usually called, succeeded his father Pepin. He was a great statesman and a great conqueror, one of his first conquests being that of the Lombards. As we have seen during the life of Pepin, the bonds between the Catholic king of the Franks and the pope had become very close. Indeed, the pope had come to regard the king of the Franks as a faithful son of the Church to whom he might turn for aid at all times.

Soon, therefore, after Charlemagne came to the throne, the pope, Adrian I, appealed to him for help against the Lombards. So across the Alps Charlemagne passed with a mighty army. In no long time the cities of Lombardy yielded to him, Pavia only holding out for six months. But that, too, fell, and Charlemagne entered in triumph into the capital of the Lombard kingdom. Desiderius, the last king of the Lombards, was taken prisoner, his head was shaved, and he was sent to France, there to end his days in a monastery.

Thus the rule of the Lombards in Italy, which had lasted for two hundred years, came to an end. But unlike his father, Charlemagne did not hand over all his conquests to the pope. He placed the crown of Lombardy on his own head, added the kingdom to his already great territory, and henceforth called himself king of the Franks and of Lombardy.

But greater than Charlemagne's conquest of the Lombards was his conquest of the Saxons. At this date a large part of what is now Germany was still pathless forest and swamp, inhabited by wild heathen Saxons. Now Charlemagne's great desire was to bring all German peoples into one Christian empire. He dreamt of a great Germanic empire in which the people would speak one language, worship one God, and obey one ruler. So he determined upon the conquest of the Saxons.

But to conquer the Saxons was no easy matter. Year by year, when spring came, with dogged determination Charlemagne set forth to attack them in their strongholds, and having, as he thought, subdued and converted them, he returned home. But year by year, with equally dogged determination, as soon as he was gone the Saxons rose in rebellion. They slew the priests and governors he had left among them, burned the churches he had built, and returned once more to the worship of their gloomy heathen gods.

For thirty years the struggle lasted. But not unlike the Mohammedans, Charlemagne was determined to convert the world, even at the sword's point if need be. So by thousands he slew the Saxons. By thousands he baptized them. He made cruel laws against those who clung to their heathen faith, or those who dared to return to it after they had been "converted" and baptized by force. He carried thousands of men, women, and children away from their homes, and planted colonies of them in France.

Thus, with the harshest and most cruel of methods, he forced the religion of love and brotherly kindness upon his fellow-men. And at length the Saxons submitted, and all Germany as far as the Elbe was added to Charlemagne's kingdom.

Charlemagne fought, too, with the pirate Danes of the north, with Slavs and Avars in the east, and with the Saracens of Spain. But although by these campaigns he added to his territory or his fame, none of his conquests were so important as those over the Lombards and the Saxons.

Missi Dominici

Besides being a great conqueror Charlemagne was also a great statesman. As a conqueror he was terrible, but once a people submitted to him he became a wise and tolerant ruler. He allowed the conquered peoples to a great extent to keep their own customs and laws, and often he appointed a native chief as their duke or ruler.

His greatest institution, perhaps, was that of the Missi Dominici or king's messengers. These king's messengers were officers whom he sent into all parts of his kingdom to see that the laws were kept and that no one suffered injustice, to listen to complaints, and generally to attend to all matters in connection with the state.

In spring each year Charlemagne held a great parliament, which, from the time of year, was called the Mayfield. To this the king's messengers came, bringing with them their reports. Thus, although

Charlemagne's kingdom was so large that he could not himself visit every portion of it every year, through his messengers he learnt what was going on in each part of it, and could thus keep it under control.

Another of Charlemagne's great works was the institution of schools. When he came to the throne there was hardly a school throughout the length and breadth of his kingdom, and he himself could neither read nor write. But he knew how important a thing learning was, so he encouraged it in every way possible.

As there were no learned men among the Franks, Charlemagne sought them from other countries, offering them large rewards if they would come to teach his people. Many answered his call, but none among them helped him so much as the Englishman, Alcuin of York. He became master of the school which Charlemagne founded in his own palace, and of which Charlemagne himself was a pupil.

Besides this one in the palace many other schools were founded throughout the kingdom, in connection with the churches and monasteries. In these not only the sons of noblemen but the sons of freemen and others of lesser degree learned to read and write. Libraries also were founded, so that those who learned to love literature might not be utterly destitute of books to read. For in those days, one must remember, few private people could afford to possess books. They were all written by hand upon vellum or parchment, and were often beautifully decorated with coloured initials and pictures. Writing or copying a book was slow work, so there were comparatively few to be had, and they cost a great deal of money.

Both in peace and war Charlemagne was the greatest figure of his times. His fame and power far surpassed that of the emperor. Either in war or peace he had dealings and with all the chief rulers of Europe. It is said that he even sent embassies to the great caliph of Bagdad, or Harun Alraschid, or Harun the Just, who is best known to Europe through the "Arabian Nights." He little deserved his surname, being in truth a cruel tyrant caring nothing for the happiness of his people. He was constantly at war with the Empire, but he received the embassies of the "Christian dog" with at least outward politeness and sent him rich gifts, among them an elephant, the first ever seen in the land of the Franks.

Charlemagne ruled in Italy as the emperors had never done since the days of Justinian. And as years went on the idea that Italy owed any fealty to the emperor faded more and more from the minds of the people, while, at the same time, an enmity between pope and emperor grew.

Iconoclasts and the Eastern Empire

Quarrels had arisen between the Church of the East and the Church of the West. The eastern bishops condemned the use of images, and wished to have them abolished; the pope upheld their use and denounced the emperor as a heretic, because it was he who instigated the bishops. Those who wished to banish images from the churches were called Iconoclasts, or image-breakers.

The war between the Iconoclasts and the Catholics waged fiercely. Then there came a revolution in Constantinople. The beautiful bad Empress Irene caused her son the Emperor Constantine VI to be blinded, and herself usurped the throne. But although the people cheered her and acclaimed her Augusta, as she drove through the streets in her gilded chariot, there were many who were filled with anger because a woman sat upon the throne of the Cæsars.

Among these was the pope, and even although Irene had restored the use of images in the churches, his wrath against her was not appeased. He became more unwilling than ever to acknowledge any allegiance to the Empire, and at length he took a step which wiped away the last pretence of it.

About this time documents, which are called the False Decretals, and the Constitutium Constantini, or the Donation of Constantine, became known to the public. They have been proved to be forgeries, but upon them much of the power of the popes was founded. For, by the Donation of Constantine, it was said that Constantine the Great had given to Pope Silvester and his successors the sovereignty of all Italy when he built his new capital on the Bosphorus. This he had done, it was said, out of gratitude to the Church, because on being baptized he had been cured of leprosy. By this Donation the popes were clearly freed from all overlordship of the emperors, who had of late proved themselves but poor champions of Italy, and the way was left open for the popes to choose a stronger staff to lean upon.

Coronation of Charlemagne

Toward the end of the year 800 Charlemagne paid a visit to Rome, and on Christmas Day, with a gorgeous train of knights and nobles, he went to the Church of St. Peter to hear mass. The great church, already five centuries old, was filled to overflowing. Beneath the light of numberless candles, gold and gems gleamed and glittered, priests in rich robes moved silently hither and thither, and the sound of sweet singing rose and fell.

Mass was over. But the king still knelt on the steps of the altar, and a breathless silence held the great congregation. Then, as the king rose from his knees, Pope Leo III came towards him holding a golden crown high in his hands, and placed it upon the monarch's head.

"To Charles Augustus, crowned by God, mighty and pacific Emperor, be life and victory," he cried.

The crowd took up the words, and three times the great building rang with acclamations. Then came an outburst of song, and in chant after chant the voices of the choristers rose, beseeching God and His angels, and all the holy martyrs, to bless and aid the new-crowned emperor.

The Holy Roman Empire

Thus began the Holy Roman Empire which was to endure for a thousand years and be shattered at length by an upstart Corsican soldier.

Was Charlemagne surprised and not altogether pleased to find this great title thus suddenly thrust upon him? Who can say? "Had I known what Leo was about to do," he said later, "I would never have entered St. Peter's on that Christmas morning." Yet for many years his thought had turned to some such title. Perhaps, however, he wished to take it at his own time, and of his own free will, and not to have it thrust upon him by an officious pope. Perhaps he saw that this act conferred more power upon the pope than honour upon the emperor, and that the time might come (as come it did) when no king of the Germans would dare to take the title of emperor until the crown had been placed upon his head by the bishop of Rome.

When the news of this coronation reached Constantinople there was great wrath, and Charlemagne's right to take the title of Augustus was denied. But Charlemagne did his best to soothe the wrath. He tried to arrange marriages between his own family and the Empress Irene, and thus again unite the Empires of the East and West. But these efforts came to nothing, and less than two years after Charlemagne was crowned emperor Irene was deposed and soon after died.

THE TREATY OF VERDUN—THE BEGINNING OF
FRANCE, ITALY, AND GERMANY

Charlemagne ruled as an emperor for more than thirteen years, during which time three emperors sat upon the Byzantine throne. With them all Charlemagne endeavoured to keep peace, sending them embassies, and calling them brother; but it was not until the year 812 that the Emperor Michael formally recognized Charlemagne's right to the imperial title.

Then for hundreds of years there were two emperors, one in the East and one in the West, each claiming to be the rightful heir of the Cæsars.

But although in the West the title of emperor endured, Charlemagne's Empire fell to pieces soon after his death, the whole state being filled with discord and violence. For it was built upon no solid foundation, but upon the will of one man.

The Sons of Louis the Pious

Charlemagne had many sons, but only one survived him. He is known as Louis the Pious, and was more fitted for the cloister than the throne. Even in his lifetime his unruly sons tried to rend the Empire from him, and after his death they quarrelled among themselves over their inheritance. After a time the two younger of these sons, Louis and Charles, joined together against Lothaire, the elder.

At Strasburg they met together, and swore an oath of eternal friendship. The taking of this oath was made an occasion of solemn ceremony. The two armies were drawn up facing each other upon the plain, and in the space between the kings, in gorgeous robes, glittering with gold and jewels, met. Each made a speech, and then with great solemnity swore to stand by the other.

Louis, being the elder, spoke first. "For the love of God," he said, "and for this Christian people and our common salvation, as much as God gives me to know and to do, I will aid my brother Charles in all things as one ought rightly to aid one's brother, on condition that he does as much for me. And I will never willingly make any compact with Lothaire which may injure this my brother Charles."

Louis repeated the same words but in another language. For the interesting thing about this oath is that it was taken in two languages. It had been the dream of Charlemagne's life to unite all the Germans under one sceptre, so that they should be one people, speaking one language, and owning one ruler.

Before he died he had even begun to write a German grammar. But already, less than thirty years after his death, there were two such widely differing languages spoken within the Empire that the Frankish soldiers of Charles and the Saxon soldiers of Louis could not understand each other. So Louis, speaking to his brother's Franks, spoke their language, and Charles, addressing the Saxon soldiers, used another language.

Out of those two languages have grown modern French and modern German.

You may see how they have developed from the few words from the beginning of the oath which follow:

Old French: "Pro Deo amur et pro Christian poble et nostro commun salvament."

Modern French: "Pour l'amour de Dieu, et pour le salut commun du peuple cretien et le notre."

Old German: "In Godes Minna ind in thes Christianes folches ind unser bedhero gehaltnissi."

Modern German: "Aus Liebe zu Gott und des Christlicher Volkes sowie unser beider Heiles halber."

Those of you who know Latin can see at once what a strong influence that language had on the French spoken in the ninth century. The Vandals and the Goths, who had, in turn, conquered Gaul, left no trace even on the language. The Franks left little, and to-day there are not more than a thousand words of Germanic origin in the whole French language. Still fewer words can be traced to Celtic—the original language of the Gauls. Latin, the language of the Romans, is the chief element. Therefore

38

we call it a Romance language—that is, one founded upon and developed from the language spoken by the ancient Romans. Italian and Spanish are also Romance languages, for in spite of repeated conquests by Vandals, Goths, Lombards, and Saracens, Latin remained the chief element in them.

Latin, on the other hand, had little influence on the German language, which is merely a development of the old German tongue. Germany never came under the civilizing influences of Rome, and its language, among other things, has remained the most primitive and undeveloped language in Europe.

The Treaty of Verdun

In the Strasburg oath we see the beginnings of modern French and of modern German. In the following year we see the beginnings of the separate existence of the two countries. For then all three brothers met together once more and signed the treaty known as the Treaty of Verdun, by which they agreed to divide the Empire. Lothaire, being the eldest, kept the title of Emperor, and to him was given Italy and a strip of land west of the Rhine, running right through the Empire, from the Mediterranean to the North Sea.

The land which lay east of this was given to Louis, and the land which lay west of it was given to Charles. Save that the two kingdoms were divided by the strip of land belonging to Lothaire, the land of Charles took roughly the form of the France of to-day, that of Louis the form of Germany. Here, then, we have the beginnings of three great states— France, Germany, and Italy.

Nearly four hundred years had passed since the last Roman emperor of the West had been swept from his throne by an audacious Teuton. And in the turmoil of these centuries it would seem as if the Teutons had brought nothing in their train but bloodshed and discord and the destruction of art and learning. But to the reforming of Europe out of the fragments of the shattered Roman Empire the Teutons brought something new.

In Rome the state was everything, the individual nothing. There was a great gulf between the powerful wealthy and the powerless poor, between the slave and the slave-owner. The slave-owner was almighty, the slave a mere chattel. But among the Teutons there were no slaves. They were a free people, and each man was conscious of his own personal worth in the community. The idea of this individual freedom was the Teutonic bequest to future ages. But in the torn fragments of the Roman Empire out of which new nations were being hammered, side by side with this idea of personal freedom there grew up another power which was, to a great extent, to nullify it. This was the papal power.

For many centuries in all the states of southern Europe the power of the Church was supreme. Only in the island of Britain, separated from the continent of Europe by the narrow seas, the power of the pope was never felt in its full force. It was there, therefore, that this idea of freedom was allowed to grow with least opposition, and at length developed fully.

THE COMING OF THE NORTHMEN

IN the last chapter we saw the dim beginnings of France, Italy, and Germany. But hundreds of years were to pass before these kingdoms really became settled. The period which followed the Treaty of Verdun was one of constant turmoil and bloodshed, for the kings were often feeble, sometimes bad, and their subjects were turbulent and rebellious. Even a strong king had endless difficulties to face.

First, there was the lack of roads. One of the first things the Romans did in a conquered country was to build roads. They knew that roads were great conquerors and great civilizers. But the barbarians who split up the Roman Empire did not know the value of roads, so the wonderful Roman highways were allowed to fall into disrepair. In Saxony, which the Romans had never conquered, there were no roads at all. The difficulties, therefore, of travelling from one part of the kingdom to another were immense, the transport of an army extremely difficult. Without roads, too, commerce languished.

Secondly, the king was almost always poor, for the system of taxation was very imperfect. Being unable quickly to travel all over the kingdom himself, the king was obliged to depute much of his authority to dukes and counts. Having little money, he paid them for their services in land, and their possessions often became so great that they were really more powerful than the king himself, and rebelled against his authority. So civil wars were constant.

Besides these and other internal disturbances, there were frequent attacks from without to be repelled, and these alone were enough to prevent Europe from settling into peace.

Soon after the death of Charlemagne the Saracens seized the island of Sicily, overran a great part of the south of the Italian Peninsula, and even threatened Rome itself. Avars and Hungarians from the wilds of Asia swept over Germany and northern Italy, and reached even to the borders of France, and at length settled in the land which is now called Hungary. And lastly, there came the Northmen. They were the last of the German tribes to attack the civilization of Europe, and they left more impression on it than almost any other, although they themselves became absorbed in the peoples they conquered.

The Home of the Northmen

Of their early history we know little or nothing. For while in southern and central Europe new kingdoms were being hammered out of the old Roman Empire, Europe beyond the Baltic was a region unknown. Until the end of the eighth century we know almost nothing of Scandinavia. Nearly all the Teutonic tribes, it is true, who took possession of the Empire came, or had traditions of having come, from the far north. They came from beyond the sluggish sea where dwelt a mighty people well skilled in the building of boats; they came "from the edge of the world." But little was known of this far-distant country.

Those of you who have read the "Germania" of Tacitus may remember how he speaks of these northern peoples and their land. "They live on islands in the sea," he says. "Their strength lies not in military forces only, but also in their ships. . . . Beyond the islands there is another sea which is sluggish, and nearly always still. It is believed to encircle the earth, for here the light of the setting sun lasts until the sun rises again, and the light is bright enough to make pale the stars. Moreover, it is said that you can hear the sea hiss as the sun rises out of it and see the god's face, and the halo about his head. This is the end of the world, it is said, and it may well be so."

The Northmen as Raiders

Hundreds of years passed, and people knew little more about this strange northern country than they did in the time of Tacitus. At length, however, towards the end of the eighth century, driven by poverty and the necessity of finding new homes, or merely by the love of adventure, the heathen Northmen began to sail forth from their bays and fiords, and attack the Christian kingdoms of Europe. They came from what are now Norway, Sweden, and Denmark, but in those days men called them all indiscriminately, Danes, Northmen, Vikings, or men of the bays and fiords. The English chronicles generally call them Danes, the French chronicles generally call them Northmen. But, by whatever name they were known, they made themselves for a hundred years the terror of seaboard Europe.

For the attacks of the Northmen differed from those of any other barbarian people in that they came from the sea, and not from the land. They sailed in long, narrow vessels, capable of holding fifty or sixty men. Bow and stern were alike, so that the ship could be steered either way, and they were decorated with the head of a swan or dragon, or some other animal. But the dragon was the favourite. Rowers sat along the sides of the vessels, and there was also one large sail.

Used as we are now to great sea-going monsters, the Viking ships seem the merest cockle-shells, and we marvel how men could venture forth upon the stormy North Sea in such frail craft. But venture forth they did, even upon the pathless ocean, and there seems now little doubt that five hundred years before Columbus the hardy Norsemen had landed upon the shores of North America.

These dragon-ships became the pest of the seas and a terror to all seaboard dwellers. It was a new terror, too. For hitherto there had been peace upon the seas. Huns, Avars, Bulgars, Goths, Vandals, Franks, Lombards, and all the other lesser tribes which had swept over Europe in turn, had made their attacks by land. Except for Saracen or Vandal pirates, the seas had still remained the peaceful routes of trade. Now that was changed. War and bloodshed came from the sea, just when it seemed as if the beginnings of peace might dawn on land.

The sea was the Northman's element. Yet, born sailor although he was, he seemed equally at home on land, where he proved himself a skilful, cunning, and absolutely cold-blooded fighter. They were blue-eyed, fair-haired, tall, and sinewy men. They wore their hair in long plaits, and dressed in gay colours, scarlet being much loved by them. They wore coats of mail and great horned helmets, and were armed with bow and arrows, hatchet, spear, and sword.

They loved war and the ways of war and the weapons of war. Their songs were all of war and the mighty blows of heroes, and in these songs they gave poetic names to their ships and weapons. But more than any other weapon they loved their swords, and to them they gave the most poetic names, such as "the lightning of war," "the thorn of shields," "the helmet biter." The hilts and scabbards of these swords were often beautifully inlaid with gold and studded with jewels, and were handed on from hero to hero, and prized as no other gift was prized.

Armed, then, at all points, these joyous, blood-thirsty pirates set forth in their dragon-ships. Along the sides they hung their gaily painted

43

shields, ringed and bossed with metal, and leaning upon their spears, they stood in the prow, while the short oars flashed, and the wind sang through the sail. When storm winds blew and others sought the shelter of the shore, the dragon-ship sped forth, spurning as if in joy the foaming waves. Then, as day dawned, some sleeping village would hear the Viking battle-cry. Then bright swords gleamed, and sparing neither man nor woman, these Northmen plundered at will. At length, their fury and their greed sated, they mounted into their ship once more and sped away as swiftly as they had come, leaving behind them only smoking, blood-stained ruins where, but a few hours before, peaceful homes had stood.

The first of these attacks of which we have any record was upon England, towards the end of the eighth century. But soon England, Scotland, Ireland, France, Germany, Spain, and Italy all knew and dreaded the terrible Northmen. Their coasts were dotted with ruins, the bones of the dead lay bleaching on a thousand battlefields, and a new petition was added to men's prayers, "From the fury of the Northmen, good Lord deliver us."

THE NORTHMEN IN FRANCE
AND ENGLAND

The Northmen as Settlers

AT the beginning of their raids the Northmen only came to plunder, and made no attempt to settle in the lands they attacked. But as time went on they came not only to plunder but to settle. And wherever they settled a change came over them. They were so adaptable that they lost their individuality and became merged in the native population. They settled in England and became Englishmen, they settled in France and became Frenchmen. Later, these Norman-French conquered England and again, in time, became Englishmen.

But before they finally settled there the attacks of the Northmen on France were both many and cruel. It was not the coasts only that they left desolate, for in their narrow vessels they sailed up the rivers, and towns and villages far inland were laid in ruins. Even Paris itself was threatened by them more than once.

The Carolingian line was by this time dying out in feebleness, and weak kings, unable to punish the impudent invaders, paid them gold to depart. The Northmen accepted the gold, but they always returned again, each time in greater and greater numbers, ever more greedy, more bold, and more cruel than before. With sword and firebrand they laid waste the land until there were whole districts in the most fertile parts of France where it was said a man might wander for long days without seeing the smoke of a chimney or hearing the bark of a dog.

"The heathen, like wolves in the night, seize upon the flocks of Christ," wails a writer of the time. "Churches are burned, women are led away captive, the people are slain. Everywhere there is mourning. From all sides cries and lamentations assail the ears of the king who, by his indolence, leaves his Christian folk to perish."

Rollo settles in the North of France

After a time, some of the Northmen, under their leader, Rollo, took possession of a part of France and settled there. And from this new base they launched even fiercer attacks on the rest of the country. At length, in the time of Charles the Simple, the French saw that to buy the Northmen off was worse than useless, and to expel them now that they were firmly rooted impossible. The only thing to do was to change lawless freebooters into law-abiding citizens.

Charles, therefore, sent messengers to the rough, old sea king, offering him the undisputed possession of all that north-west portion of France in which he and his warriors had already settled. In return for this, he was to become a Christian, be baptized, and own himself vassal of the king. Rollo was not unwilling to listen to the king's proposal, but he was not content with the land offered to him.

"The land is desolate and barren," he said, "there is not there the wherewithal to live." So he demanded more land. Thereupon the king offered him Flanders. For he had a grudge against the count of Flanders. But Rollo would have none of it.
"It is nothing but a waste of bog and marsh," he said, and he demanded Brittany.

Now the part of France called Brittany had never really been in the possession of the kings of France. So all Charles could give Rollo was the right to conquer it, if he could. And this he readily gave.

Matters being thus settled, Rollo had next to perform his part of the compact, and do homage as a vassal. Upon the appointed day the king seated himself upon his throne with his priests and courtiers about him, and to him came the rough old Northman and his warriors. The ceremony began, but when Rollo was told that he must kneel before the king and kiss his feet he started back in wrath.

"No, by Heaven!" he cried. "I will kiss no man's feet!

"It must be," replied the priests, "in no other way can you hold your fief."

"Then let one of my followers do it for me," replied the proud sea-king.

And as nothing would move Rollo, Charles had to be content with that. So one of Rollo's followers was bidden to perform the act of homage for his master. But he had as little liking as Rollo for what seemed to him a piece of degrading foolery. He had never bent his knee to any man, and he did not mean to do it now. Striding, therefore, up to the throne, without even bending, he seized the king's foot and raised it to his mouth. So rough and sudden was his action that Charles fell backwards to the ground. And thus, amid the loud laughter not only of the rude Northmen but of the Frankish courtiers also, the strange ceremony of homage ended.

After this Rollo was duly baptized, and received the Christian name of Robert, and many of his warriors followed his example and were baptized also. Their conversion was sudden. But this was nothing to the Northmen. For it was said many of them made an annual practice of it, merely for the sake of the white linen robe which they received on the occasion.

The land which was thus given to Rollo was already known as Northmannie. It soon became Normandy, and its people Normans. Very quickly they forgot their heathen religion and their northern speech and northern home. Normandy, strange to say, became the best governed part of France, and the exploits of Rollo the Ganger, the devastator of France, the pillager of monasteries, the slayer of women and children, were almost forgotten in the fame of Robert, Duke of Normandy, the builder of churches, and framer of righteous laws.

Outwardly, wherever the Northmen settled they seemed to disappear and be merged in the native population. In reality they imbued these populations with something of their own spirit. They were filled with a great curiosity, they had a genius for order and government, they were fearless, energetic, and eager, always ready to adventure and to do. Civilized, they retained much of the old vigour which as barbarian heathen had made them such deadly and pitiless foes. Christianized, they became the passionate champions of the Catholic Church. And the descendants of those Vikings who had refused to bend the knee to any man, and laughed aloud at the discomfiture of their over-lord, became the great upholders of the feudal system, the impassioned exponents of the orders of knighthood and chivalry.

The Northmen in England

England suffered from the Northmen even as did France. Here, however, they were met and checked by a skilful soldier and statesman, Alfred the Great. Yet even he, with all his courage and perseverance, could not altogether loosen the grip of the Northmen upon the island. At length he, too, like the king of France, was obliged to buy peace by yielding part of his kingdom to the freebooters. And, by the Peace of Wedmore, Alfred assigned to the Danes all the northern half of England. The conditions of this treaty were similar to those upon which Rollo acquired Normandy. Guthrun the Dane was baptized, receiving the name of Athelstane and owning Alfred as overlord.

But with the Peace of Wedmore the struggle in England did not cease. It was only abated. During the rest of Alfred's life and for more than a century after his death it continued, until in 1016 Knut the Dane became king of all England. This Northman domination lasted until 1042, ending only fourteen years before the conquest of England by William the Norman.

THE BEGINNING OF RUSSIA

THE conquest of England by the Northmen and their settlement in France, out of which arose the second conquest of England, are the most important results of the "Northman Fury" for western Europe. In eastern Europe the most important result was the founding of Russia.

About the middle of the ninth century some Northmen, Swedes in all probability, sailed east, just as their brethren sailed west and south, upon a marauding expedition. They made a settlement on the shores of the Gulf of Finland, and laid the Slavonic tribes along the coast under tribute. After a time, however, the Slavs succeeded in driving out these invaders. But having got rid of them the Slavs fell to quarrelling among themselves. "There was no more justice among them," says an old chronicle. "Family disputed with family, so that they fell to war." At length the turmoil and bloodshed became so great that some among them were fain to confess that the domination of the Northmen was more endurable than the misrule of their own princes.

"Let us seek a prince," they said, "who will judge us according to the right." Therefore they sent messengers to the Northmen, begging them to return. "Our land is large and fertile," they said, "but it is filled with discord and clamour. Come, then, and rule over us."

Rurick settles in Russia

In answer to this petition the Viking Rurick, with his two brothers, came to settle in what is now Russia. These Northmen were often called Varangians or Varingars. No one is sure how they got this name, but it is believed to be Arabian in origin. The Arabians, at least, called all the northern peoples Varangians, whether they invented the name or not. But the people who lived in Finland called them the Rousses, and soon the Slav subjects of Rurick came to be called Russians and their country Russia. Rous in Finnish to-day means a Swede. So it seems probable that the name of the greatest Slavonic people is of Finnish, and not of Slavonic origin.

Rurick made his capital at Novgorod, and two years after his settlement there his brothers died, and he became sole ruler of the province. We know very little of his government or whether the people lived to regret having called in a foreigner to rule over them. But it is said that after a time two Viking warriors, one named Askold and one named Dir, became discontented with his rule. So, taking several companions with them, they left Novgorod, and set out to seek their fortunes at Constantinople. On their way they came upon a castle on the banks of the Dnieper, with a small town round it.

"Whose castle is this?" they asked of the inhabitants.

"It was built by three brothers," replied they, "but they are long since dead. We are their descendants, and pay tribute to the Khazars."

Hearing that, Askold and Dir took possession of the town, which was called Kief. They were soon joined by other Northmen, and thus a second Viking settlement was made in Russia.

This second settlement soon increased, and then, with true Viking audacity and love of adventure, they made up their minds to attack Constantinople. Dwelling far inland although they now were, these Northmen had not forgotten their skill as sailors. Soon two hundred dragon-headed boats went sailing down the Dnieper and out into the Black Sea, and ere long the terrified inhabitants of Constantinople saw, for the first time, the gay sails and long narrow boats of the dreaded Northmen.

The Greeks were paralysed with fear. Nothing but a miracle, it seemed, could save them from destruction. The miracle happened, for a sudden storm arose which shattered the Viking ships, only a miserable remainder of which, like wounded birds, crept slowly back to Kief.

Prince Igor and Oleg

For some time the two Northman settlements in Russia remained separate from each other. But after ruling for fifteen years in the northern settlement Rurick died. His son, Igor, was only a boy, so Rurick left his kinsman Oleg as regent.

Far more than Rurick, Oleg was filled with the desire of conquest, and he resolved to bring both the northern and southern settlements under one rule. He knew, however, that Askold and Dir were not likely to give up their kingship without a struggle, and he had recourse, therefore, to treachery.

With a great fleet of boats he sailed down the Dnieper. Then as they neared Kief, leaving his soldiers behind him, he went on with the young Prince Igor, and a few soldiers only, hidden in the bottom of his boat. Arrived at Kief, he sent messengers to Askold and Dir, saying that Northman merchants passing on their way to Constantinople desired to greet them in the name of the Prince of Novgorod.

Askold and Dir, suspecting no treachery, at once hurried to the river bank, only to find themselves surrounded by Viking warriors, and led captive before Oleg.

"You are no princes," he said to them, haughtily. "You are not even of noble birth. As for me, I am a prince." Then, taking Igor by the hand, he led him forward.

"Behold the son of Rurick!" he cried.

It was the signal agreed upon, and at the words the Vikings fell upon Askold and Dir and slew them. Then, his hands still red with blood, Oleg marched in triumph into Kief. Everything that he saw there delighted the old warrior. It seemed to him, with the Dnieper flowing by, a splendid point from which to lead his warriors forth to conquest, and he resolved to make his capital there. "This town shall be the mother of all Russian towns!" he cried.

Such is the more or less legendary story of the founding of Russia by the Vikings, and for many a long day the rulers traced their descent to the sea-king Rurick.

Meanwhile, more than twenty years passed during which Oleg extended his conquests all around, and added province after province to his kingdom. But he kept peace with the Eastern Empire, and a regular trade route was established from the shores of the Baltic to the Golden Horn. Along this route there came many a peaceful merchant, bringing furs from the snowy north, and carrying back with him in exchange the corn and wine of the south. Thus numbers of Russians came to know of Myklegaard or the Great City, as they called Constantinople. To these rude, northern giants the riches and luxury they saw there were a constant wonder and amaze, and they carried home with them strange tales of its marvels.

So at length, either driven on by his peoples' envy of the riches of the Eastern Empire, or desirous of finding a foeman worthy of his steel, Oleg decided to attack Constantinople, and gathering a great host of warriors, he set out. For many a mile the River Dnieper was covered with boats, two thousand in all, it is said, while vast squadrons of horsemen accompanied them along the banks. Seeing them come in such force the Greeks fled within their city, put a chain across the harbour, and left the wild Northmen to plunder and burn at will in all the country around. The desolation they made was truly terrible, for in becoming Russian the Northmen had lost none of their Viking fury.

But Oleg was bent on taking the city itself. So he ordered his soldiers to make wheels, and placing his boats upon them, he brought them overland right up to the walls of Constantinople. When the Greeks saw this strange sight their last vestige of courage gave way, and sending messengers to the Russians, they begged for peace. "Spare our city," they said, "and we will give you all the tribute you demand."

To this Oleg agreed, and having received an immense ransom, he made a treaty of peace with the emperor. As the emperor swore to keep the peace he kissed the Cross, but Oleg swore by his sword, for he was a heathen, as most of his people still were. Then, having hung his sword on the gates of Constantinople as a sign of his victory, he returned home, richly laden with booty.

But peace between the Empire and Russia did not last. For Constantinople had proved a rich and easy prey, and four times at least in less than two hundred years the Russians appeared before its walls, and forced the emperor to buy them off.

With all their growing power the Russian rulers did not take the regal title, but called themselves Grand Dukes. In 980 Vladimir I became Grand Duke. He was a fratricide, a heathen, and an evil liver. But he was a great soldier and a wise statesman. He desired, above all things to make his country great, and he believed that an alliance with the Empire would serve his purpose better than war. So he asked the emperors, Basil II and Constantine VII, to give him the hand of their sister Anne in marriage. But the emperors refused to give their sister in marriage to a heathen.

"Be baptized," they said, "and you shall marry our sister." Vladimir immediately promised to do as they wished, whereat the emperors rejoiced. But the Princess Anne wept bitter tears.

"You send me to slavery among a heathen people!" she cried. "It is worse than death."

"Not so, sister," replied the emperors, "it is by thee that God will lead the Russian nation to penitence, and thou wilt save the Empire from a cruel war."

So Vladimir was baptized, and the marriage between him and the Grecian princess was celebrated with great rejoicings and splendour. Then Vladimir caused every idol in Kief to be destroyed and cast into the river, and commanded all his people on pain of his displeasure to be baptized at once. Many obeyed him. "For," said they, "the religion must be good, or our prince would not have accepted it."

The Greek Church

Thus was Christianity introduced into Russia. For although many years before priests had come from Constantinople to teach the people about the true God, only few had listened to them. Thus, too, it comes about that the Russians, to this day, belong to the Greek and not to the Roman Church.

After this time there was great intercourse between the Empire and Russia, and the emperors formed a bodyguard of Northmen whom they called the Varangian guard, These Varangians were bound to the emperor by a special oath. They lived in the palace itself, one of their special duties being to guard the door of the emperor's bedchamber. They were accorded many privileges, and it was considered a great honour to serve in the guard of Myklegaard. Besides this special guard many Northmen were to be found among the soldiers and sailors of the Empire, and many Vikings of fame came to serve the emperor.

With Vladimir the Viking period of Russian history ends, and Russia begins to take a place among the Christian states of Europe. Besides the alliance with the emperor, the Grand Dukes of Russia soon made alliances with France and other of the great states of Europe. But the country was constantly torn asunder by civil wars. Rival princes claimed the title and authority of grand duke, little princedoms sprang up, and were crushed out of existence again. So instead of consolidating into a kingdom the country remained merely a conglomeration of rival principalities, until in the thirteenth century the Mongols, taking advantage of this disunion, conquered the country and held it in subjection for more than two hundred years.

THE NORMAN KINGDOM OF SICILY

The Saracens in Sicily

THE same restless energy which drove the Northmen out of their native country drove the Normans out of Normandy, and led them to seek adventures in other lands. And how, even before William of Normandy conquered England, a Norman adventurer made himself ruler of Sicily is one of the most picturesque chapters of European history.

Sicily at this time was, in theory, still part of the Eastern Empire. In reality it had long been in the possession of the Saracens, who had also overrun the southern states of the Italian Peninsula. These states were, at the same time, full of internal unrest, their petty chiefs frequently quarrelling with each other. They were, as well, a bone of contention between the Emperor of the West and the Emperor of the East, who each claimed them as part of his Empire, while the pope also had his eye upon them.

We find the Greeks now fighting against Saracens, now trying to subdue some native rebellious chief. Now Greek Emperor and German Emperor join against the Saracens, or again, Greeks and Saracens join in routing the Germans. In the general turmoil there was room enough for the adventurous free-lance. Norman adventurers travelled far and were always ready to lend their swords to any side which would pay them, and just as ready to change sides. And ere long we find them taking part in the fray.

Chief among these Norman adventurers were the sons of Tancred of Hauteville. They were "of middling parentage, neither very low nor very high." There were twelve brothers, among whom William of the Iron Arm, Robert Guiscard, or the Wily, Humphrey, and Roger are the most famous. There was no scope for their ardent and ambitious spirits in their native village, so they set forth to seek their fortune by their swords. They "journeyed through divers places, in military fashion, seeking gain, and at last, by God's providence, reached Apulia, a province of Italy."

Robert Guiscard

Soon we find Iron Arm and Humphrey, with their followers, in the service of the Greek Emperor, helping to rout the Saracens. But when the fight was over, and the spoil was divided, the Normans considered that they did not receive their fair share. They complained loudly, but instead of listening to their demands, the Greek general insulted their leader. Thereupon the proud adventurers determined to avenge the insult. And passing over to the mainland, they roused the Normans who had already settled there. In many battles they defeated the Greeks, and at length put an end to their rule. They won Pope Nicholas II to their cause, and at his hands Robert Guiscard received the title of duke. Thus a Norman adventurer "of middling parentage" became "Robert, by the grace of God and of St. Peter, Duke of Apulia and of Calabria, and future Duke of Sicily by their aid."

It was Roger chiefly who carried out the conquest of Sicily. But it was a long and terrible struggle. Many towns were laid in ruins, and much blood was shed before Norman rule was established in the island. In 1072, indeed, Robert gave his brother Roger the title of Count of Sicily, but it was nearly twenty years later before the last town submitted to him. Long ere this Robert Guiscard was dead, and his son Roger Borsa ruled as duke. At the good age of seventy Roger the great count also died, and was succeeded by his son, also called Roger. This Roger made up his mind to unite all the Norman conquests in Sicily and Italy under one rule. But to do this he felt that he must have the title of king.

At this time two popes, Anacletus II and Innocent II, were struggling for the papal throne. Roger supported Anacletus, and in return received from him the title of king. And on Christmas Day, 1130, he was crowned at Palermo with great magnificence. Thus Sicily began its long and chequered career as a kingdom. Yet although Roger was really the first Norman king of Sicily (his father having merely held the title of count), he is generally known as Roger II.

Roger had attained his ambition, but it cost him ten years of war. All Europe seemed to gather against him. The Emperor of the East began to fear the growing power of these upstart Normans who had wrested Sicily from the Empire. The German Emperor Lothaire, the King of France, Louis VI, the King of England, Henry I, and Pope Innocent II, all, for one reason or another, were against him, besides which there were rebels in Italy itself.

For a time Roger suffered many defeats. But in the end he

conquered, and he even induced Pope Innocent, after the 1189 death of Anacletus, to confirm him in his title of king. But the dynasty he founded did not last long, and with the death of Tancred in 1194 Norman rule in Sicily came to an end.

THE BEGINNING OF SCANDINAVIA— DENMARK AND SWEDEN

WHILE the Northmen were founding new kingdoms in Europe, the countries they had left were also taking shape. But save for a few remarks in the works of ancient writers, nothing is known of Scandinavia in early days. There are indeed many sagas or hero stories of far-off times. But although these are delightful reading, and give a wonderful insight into the habits and customs of the Northmen, they cannot be looked upon as serious history. After the Northmen began to attack Europe, the chronicles of all the countries which suffered from them are full of their dreadful doings. But there are no Scandinavian chronicles of the same period. So we do not know what was happening in the countries whence these pirates came.

ENGLAND AND THE NORTHMEN

The first mention we have of a king of Denmark is during Charlemagne's Saxon wars (see Chapter IX). Then more than once Siegfried, King of Denmark, sheltered Wittikind, the great Saxon hero, from the wrath of Charlemagne. But until the end of the tenth century Denmark and the kings of Denmark are of very little account. Up to that time it was the men who left their country in order to raid Europe, and found new kingdoms there, who mattered, and not the kings and country they left behind. So these countries come late into the story of Europe. From the time anything is known of them, they were small, and they were constantly being divided by civil wars. They seemed too insignificant to have any influence on the growth of Europe. Yet in the building up of France, England, and Russia the people of these countries played a great part.

Indeed, all Europe was their battle-field, and where they came they conquered, none daring to attack them in their northern strongholds. Only Germany cast a covetous eye on the northern peninsula, and Henry the Fowler crossed the Eider, and reduced the south of Denmark to a mere province of the Empire.

The Germans would have pushed their conquests further still had not the Viking queen Thyra roused the people, and in three years caused a wall to be built against the invader. Part of this wall may still be seen, and the queen who caused it to be built is known to this day as Thyra Danebod or Dane's Defence. She died not long after the great work was finished, and over her grave the king raised a huge mound and placed a stone upon it with the description, "Gorm the King raised this stone to the memory of Thyra, his wife. Denmark's Defence."

Knut the Great

In the reign of Sweyn Forkbeard, the kings of Denmark begin to be of some European importance. Forkbeard began the conquest of England and of Norway, and his son, Knut the Great, finished his work, and when he died was ruler of a vast northern empire.

When Knut first came to England he was a blood-thirsty pirate, burning and slaying with ruthless cruelty. But as with his countryman Rollo, with power came judgment, and the freebooter was changed into a righteous ruler, the slumbering fires of his barbarian soul only bursting into flames once and again.

Knut was a power in Europe. The greatest rulers of the time, the emperor Conrad II and the pope, he treated as equals, and neither as spiritual nor temporal superiors, and he induced the emperor to restore the land between the Eider and the Danework which had been conquered by Henry the Fowler. Thus the frontiers between Denmark and the Holy Roman Empire were restored as they had been in the time of Charlemagne, and as they were to be for more than eight hundred years. Then at length they were swept away by Prussian aggression.

But the empire of Knut, like the empire of Charlemagne, was held together merely by the will of one man. It could not endure, and when Knut died his empire fell almost immediately to pieces, and England, Denmark, Norway, and Sweden became separate kingdoms.

After Knut the reigns of the kings of Denmark are full of civil wars. In these wars the German emperors constantly took part, for they were anxious to make Denmark part of the Holy Roman Empire. They had good hope of succeeding, for Denmark was more than once divided between rival aspirants to the throne, and the many factions left the country open to the invader. But under Valdamar the Great, Denmark was again united, and became the most powerful of all northern states.

Valdamar and Absalon

In all his undertakings Valdamar was aided by the archbishop of Lund, Axel or Absalon. He was equally great as a soldier, a statesman, and a priest. When Valdamar came to the throne Denmark was wasted by civil war, and made desolate by the attacks of the Wends or Slavs, who lived round the shores of the Baltic. They were a scourge and terror to Scandinavia just as the Northmen had been to the rest of Europe two centuries earlier. Absalon was determined to clear the country of these pirates, and for ten years he fought them. After long struggle he seized their chief fortress, hewed the four-headed wooden god into firewood, and burned his temple. This struck such terror into the hearts of the pirates that the next fortress which Absalon attacked yielded without a blow. He and a few companions marched unscathed through mile-long ranks of Wendish warriors drawn up to receive them, cut the hideous seven-headed idol in pieces, and baptized the whole population at the point of the sword.

Absalon also built a fortress of defence against the attacks of the Wends. This fortress was called Kaupmanna Havn, or Merchant's Haven. To-day it is Copenhagen, the capital of Denmark, and near the spot where Absalon's castle stood his statue may now be seen.

When Valdamar died he had united Denmark, and extended his sway over many Baltic lands, and had earned for himself the title of liberator of his country and preserver of peace. His sons, Knut VI and Valdamar II followed in his steps. They increased their conquests until the Baltic was little more than a Danish lake, and Denmark became important as it had not been since the days of Knut the Great. Even the Holy Roman Empire paid toll to Valdamar II, and his rule extended as far south as Lübeck and Hamburg. But at the height of his greatness a sudden change came over his fortunes and those of his kingdom.

In 1223 he was treacherously seized by one of his German vassals, Henry of Schwerin, and carried away prisoner to the castle of Dannenberg in Germany. Here for two and a half years, in spite of all efforts towards his release, he pined, while his German vassals, following Count Henry's example, rose in rebellion. He only won his release at length by paying a huge ransom, and giving up his Baltic conquests, and the land lying between the Eider and the Elbe.

As soon as he was free Valdamar tried to retrieve his fortunes by the sword, but in the battle of Bornhoved he was utterly defeated. This might be looked upon as one of the decisive battles of history, for it put an end to Danish rule in the Baltic and Danish hopes of a northern empire.

After his defeat, with unusual wisdom, Valdamar thought no more of conquest but turned his attention to the betterment of the land which still remained to him. Thus in the last years of his reign he introduced many reforms and codified the Danish laws.

For a century after the death of Valdamar II Denmark was torn asunder by civil war, and half the kings died by violence. "At the death of Valdamar II," says an old chronicle, "the crown slipped from off the head of the Danes. Henceforward they became the laughing-stock of all their neighbours through civil wars and mutual fury, and the lands which they had honourably won by the sword were not only lost but caused great mischief to the realm and wasted it."

Union of Calmar, 1397

When Valdamar IV came to the throne Denmark had sunk to the lowest point in its history. But under him it rose again for a short time to something nearer its past greatness. When he died he had recovered much of the territory which had been lost during the previous reigns. He was succeeded by his grandson Olaf, whose mother Margaret acted as regent. She was then but twenty-two, but she is one of the greatest figures in Scandinavian history. When in 1387 Olaf died, she adopted her grand-nephew Eric. Through her influence Denmark, Norway, and Sweden were united under him by the Union of Cahalan.

Sweden

In Sweden serious history begins with the reign of Olaf Skettkonung the Lap-King. He received this name, it is said, because he was still a baby sitting in his mother's lap when his subjects came to do homage to him. He made an alliance with Knut the Great, and it may be that he joined Knut's army when first he invaded England.

Olaf introduced Christianity into Sweden. But for a long time many of the people refused to accept the new religion, and nearly eighty years later we find a Christian king, Inge, being driven from his throne, because he would not sacrifice to heathen gods. "At a thing (parliament) which the

61

Swedes held with Inge," so runs an old saga, "they offered him two things: either to follow the old faith or give up the kingship. Inge answered and said, 'I cannot reject the faith that is truest.' Whereupon the Swedes raised a cry, pelted him with stones, and drove him forth."

The king's brother-in-law Blotsweyne, so called from blota, a sacrifice, then usurped the throne, and once more set up the old heathen religion. But in less than three years Inge returned, slew Blotsweyne, and again took possession of the kingdom. With Blotsweyne's death the power of heathendom in Sweden was broken, although the worship of idols did not readily die, and in remote districts it was preserved still for many years. Indeed, Sweden was probably not really Christianized until the reign of St. Eric. He carried his religious zeal as far as Finland, conquering a great part of that country, which remained a dependency of Sweden for six and a half centuries.

During the following hundred years Sweden was cursed with tyrannical and incapable kings. Many of them came to the throne as children, and regents ruled—some well but mostly ill. There were incessant wars, both within the country and without, and these helped to make the nobles powerful and arrogant. They oppressed the people and coerced the king, who was often little more than their henchman.

In 1319 Magnus II was elected king. He was but three years old, and when his grandfather Hakon V of Norway died in the same year he became king of Norway also. But the union was one in name only. When he came of age Magnus utterly neglected Norway, and in 1355 the Norwegians chose his son Hakon as king. His wife was Margaret, daughter of King Valdamar of Denmark.

The reign of Magnus was full of disaster. The Black Death swept Scandinavia, carrying off more than a third of the population. Magnus was involved in debt and disastrous wars, and at length some nobles who had been banished by Magnus offered the throne to his brother-in-law Albert of Mecklinburg.

Then civil war raged. Albert filled the land with German favourites, who oppressed the people, and the people rose against them. German pirates swept the Baltic, and the trade of Scandinavia was ruined.

By this time King Hakon of Norway was dead, and his widow

Margaret was regent of both Norway and Denmark. To her the Swedes now appealed for help, and in 1389 Albert was defeated and taken prisoner. But still the war continued, Swedes and Germans fighting with bitter hatred. "In Sweden at this time," says an old chronicle, "there were enemies on all sides, son against father and brother against brother." At length in 1395 peace was made, and Albert was released on condition of paying an enormous ransom. Then in 1397, by the Union of Calmar, Margaret's grand-nephew Eric of Pomerania was acknowledged king of Denmark, Norway, and Sweden.

THE BEGINNING OF SCANDINAVIA—
NORWAY

Harold Haarfager

NORWAY appears in history about the same time as Denmark and Sweden. Harold Haarfager, or Harold of the Splendid Locks, conquered the petty chiefs who ruled Norway and made himself sole king. He extended his conquests far beyond Norway. Orkney and Shetland became Norwegian earldoms, and even the Isle of Man and Iceland owned his sway.

"On a summer he sailed with his host west-over-sea, and came first to Shetland, and there slew all the Vikings who might not flee before him. Then he sailed south to the Orkneys, and cleared them utterly of Vikings. And thereafter he fared right away to the South isles, and harried there, and slew many Vikings who were captains of bands there. There had he many battles, and ever gained the day. Then he harried in Scotland, and had battles there. And when he came west to Man, the folk thereof had already heard what warfare King Harold had done on the land aforetime, and all folk fled into Scotland, so that Man was a waste of men, and all the good things that might be were flitted away. So when King Harold and his folk went a-land they got no prey there." (Heimskringla).

Harold was a fierce barbarian fighter, but he had some statesmanship also. "Whensoever swift rage or anger fell on him, he held himself aback at first, and let the wrath run off him, and looked at the matter unwrathfully." He had also what was wonderful in those days, some respect for his neighbour's rights. "Harold was the greatest king in Norway, and he had to do with kings of the folk-lands, and broke them down under him; yet he knew what was meet for him, and not to covet the realm of the Swede king, and for that reason the Swede kings let him sit in peace."

He also laid a ban upon robbery in the land. Therefore, many restless malcontents left the country rather than submit to the tyranny of such laws. France, Great Britain, and Ireland suffered accordingly. Among those who sailed in quest of new lands was Rolf or Rollo Wend-afoot.

"Therefore, at a thing he gave out that he made Rolf (who would be ever a-harrying in the East-lands) an outlaw. . . . Rolf Wend-afoot fared therefor west-over-sea to the South isles. Thence west he went to Valland, and harried there, and won therein a mighty earldom, and peopled all the land with Northmen, and henceforth has that land been called Normandy."

In the end Harold ruined his work of uniting Norway by giving lesser kingships to about twenty of his sons, and each of these sons determined in his own mind to be king after his father's death. So when at the age of seventy-three Harold died, the land was once more torn by civil wars, the brothers slaying each other and wasting the realm in the contest for supremacy.

Hakon the Good

But at length Hakon the Good, Harold's youngest son, got the better of all the others, and reigned in Norway for twenty-seven years. He had been brought up at the court of Athelstane, and was therefore "a well christened man when he came to Norway."

"So he was minded when he was set fast in the land, and had gotten all to him freely to hold, he would then set forth the Christian faith. And at the beginning he wrought in such wise that he lured such as were best beloved by him to become Christians, and so much did his friendship prevail therein that very many let themselves be christened, and other some left off blood-offerings."

But when Hakon tried to force Christianity on the whole people he failed. They not only refused baptism but compelled the king to take part in their heathen sacrifices. At this Hakon was so incensed that he determined to force Christianity upon the whole people at the point of the sword. He was only held back from this by the danger which threatened his kingdom through the attacks of his nephews, who had been disappointed of their heritage.

Hakon had need of a united people to repel these attacks, so he made peace with his heathen subjects, and they joined their swords with his in defence of the realm.

In one of these battles Hakon was slain. As he lay wounded he longed for Christian burial. "Yet," he said, "if I die here amongst the heathen, then give me grave such as seemeth good unto you." So the first

Christian king of Norway was buried with heathen rites. "Such words they spake over his grave as heathen men have custom, wishing him welfare to Valhall."

Olaf Tryggvason

It was under one of Hakon's successors, Olaf Tryggvason, that Norway became Christian. In early youth he was a Viking as fierce and blood-thirsty as any. "He was a danger to the lives of the Gotland folk, and I hear he fought at Sconey. He hewed the mail coats with the sword in Denmark, and south of Heathby he cut down the vulgar carcases of the Saxons for the steeds of the witches (wolves). He gave the blood of many a Frisian to the night prowlers. He fed the wolves on the bodies of the Bretons of Gaul, and gave the flesh of the Flemings to the raven. The young king waged war against the English, and made a slaughter of the Northumbrians. He destroyed the Scots far and wide. He held a sword play in Man. The archer king brought death to the islander and to the Irish. He battled with the dwellers in the land of Wales, and cut down the Cumbrian folk." (Saga of Olaf).

In 994 Olaf invaded England with Sweyn, king of Denmark, and while there he became Christian. He promised Ethelred "that he would never more come to England with war," and he kept his promise.

The year after this visit to England he suddenly appeared in Norway, and was received as king with acclamation. Like Hakon he determined to make his people Christian. With those immediately about him he was successful. "Then fared the king into the north parts, and bade all men take christianizing, but those who gainsaid him he mishandled sorely. Some he slew, some he maimed, some he drave away from the land."

So through all his kingdom Olaf passed, and by persuasion, threats, or at the point of the sword, he forced the whole people to accept the baptism of Christ. And when the haughty Queen Sigrid, whom he wooed as his wife, refused to become a Christian, he struck her in the face with his glove and left her straightway.

"This may well be the bane of thee," she cried, and thereafter Sigrid the Haughty was King Olaf's greatest foe. She married King Sweyn of Denmark and induced him to join with Olaf of Sweden in a war against Norway to avenge her wrongs.

The ships of the allies far outnumbered those of Olaf, but he disdained to flee, and after a desperate struggle off Stralsund the Norwegians were overcome. But rather than fall into the hands of the enemy Olaf leaped into the sea and was drowned. His people, however, could not believe that he was dead. So the legend grew up that he would return again, just as the legend of Arthur grew, and later that of Barbarossa.

Olaf Haroldson or St. Olaf

In 1015 Olaf Haroldson made himself king of Norway by force of the sword; but many of the people received him gladly, for it seemed to them that Olaf Tryggvason had come again, and in popular story many of the exploits of Olaf Tryggvason are ascribed to Olaf Haroldson. Among these is the Christianizing of Norway, and after his death Olaf Haroldson was named St. Olaf, and became the patron saint of Norway. In life, however, he was a vigorous statesman and warrior.

"It was proof of his stern rule that the wardens of the land had the heads of many pirates cut short with keen weapons. . . . They that made armed trespass ofttimes offered gold to the stern king for ransom; but he refused it and commanded their heads to be chopped off with the sword. The blessed king maimed the race of robbers and reivers, thus he cut short theft, he made every chief lose hands and feet, so he bettered the peace of the land. Nor did treason thrive towards the king." (Olaf's dirge).

Knut the Great

For ten years Olaf reigned undisturbed. Then in 1025, when Knut the Great had firmly established his rule over England, he sent messengers to Olaf demanding that he should do homage to him as overlord.

"Then answered King Olaf: 'I have heard it told in ancient tales that Gorm the Dane king was deemed to be a mighty enough king of the people, and he ruled over Denmark alone; but this the Dane kings that have been since deem not enough. And now it has come to this, that Knut rules over Denmark and over England, and, moreover, has broken a mickle deal of Scotland under his sway, yet now he layeth claim to my lawful heritage at my hands. He should wot how to have measure in his grasping in the end; or is he minded alone to rule over all the North-lands? Or does he mean, he alone, to eat all kale in England? Yea, he will have might thereto or ever

I bring him my head, or give him any louting soever. Now shall ye tell him these words of mine, that I mean to ward Norway with point and edge whiles my life days last thereto, and not to pay any man scat for my own kingdom."

But Knut was minded to be emperor of the north. He was rich in men and money, so with gold and sword he invaded Norway. All those to whom Olaf's stern rule had caused discontent were easily bribed to join his foes against him, and after a short struggle he left his kingdom to the spoiler, and fled to Russia. Eighteen months later he returned to make a fight for his crown once more; but at the battle of Stiklarstad he was slain. "The Danish men had then in Norway mickle mastery, and the folk of the land were right ill-content thereat."

But on the death of Knut five years later the Norwegians made Olaf's son Magnus king and the connection with Denmark ended.

For nearly a century after this the land was more or less peaceful, then for another century, 1130 to 1240, there followed a period of civil wars, many would-be kings struggling for the crown. In 1240 the last of these claimants was killed, and better times began to dawn for the country. Then when Hakon VI, son of Magnus of Sweden, died, he was succeeded by his son Olaf, and Margaret his widow became regent, until all three Scandinavian kingdoms were united by the Union of Calmar.

THE FEUDAL SYSTEM

WHEN in 911 the pirate king, Rollo the Ganger, was transformed into Robert, Duke of Normandy (see Chapter XII) he did homage to his superior, Charles the Simple. Although, as you remember, he refused to kiss the king's feet, in all probability he, or one of his followers for him, knelt before the king, put his hands in these of the king, and vowed to be his man. This is the original meaning of homage, the word being derived from home, the French for man. We have no record of the exact ceremony performed by Rollo. But we know that some such ceremony must have taken place, for the feudal system was already in force in France. By this ceremony Rollo was installed as Duke of Normandy; but the land did not become his in absolute possession. It still belonged, in theory at least, to the king, who bestowed it on Rollo as a fief, and in accepting this fief Rollo became the vassal or servant of the king (vassalis).

To trace the rise of feudalism, or to explain all its various phases and modifications in various countries, would be impossible in a short space. Broadly, feudalism was the name given to a peculiar form of government founded on the holding of land by military service. It was a result of the wild confusion into which all the countries of western Europe were thrown upon the break-up of the Carolingian Empire (see Chapter X), and was developed partly from old Roman custom, partly from new barbarian custom.

The root idea was that all the land in a country belonged to the king, who held it from God alone; but no one man, king although he might be, could farm the land of a whole country. Therefore he gave it to whomsoever he would; but he did not give it outright, nor did he give it without recompense. The king as overlord merely gave to any man he wished to reward the use of the land during his lifetime. In return the subject promised to be faithful to his king, and to help him in his wars. This was done with solemn ceremony. Kneeling before the king the subject placed his hands within those of the king and vowed to be his man. The king then kissed and raised him to his feet, and the act of homage was complete.

Next, with his hand upon some holy relic, or upon the Gospels, the vassal took the oath of fealty, and swore to be true to his overlord. This being done, the king gave his vassal a sod of earth and the branch of a tree as a sign that he was now in possession of the land for which he had done homage. It was only the great vassals or vassals-in-chief who received their land directly from the king. They, in their turn, divided their land, and granted it in fiefs to lesser lords, who did homage not to the king but to them. They again divided their land among still lesser lords. And so it went on, from highest to lowest, from the king who, in theory, possessed all the land down to the poor knight who did homage to some petty lord for a few acres.

Besides undertaking to furnish him with a certain number of soldiers in time of war, the vassal had other obligations towards his lord. The chief of these were the aids. These aids were sums of money which the overlord had the right to ask on four occasions: namely, upon the knighting of his eldest son, upon the marriage of his eldest daughter, upon his departure for a Crusade, and for his own ransom, should he happen to be taken prisoner in battle. The vassal was bound to come when called upon to help his lord with advice.

In theory a vassal was put in possession of a fief for his lifetime only; but, as a matter of fact, fiefs descended from father to son. For when a holder died his eldest son did homage for the fief and swore fealty to his overlord as his father had done before him. If, however, a holder died without direct heirs, then the fief returned into the possession of the overlord. Or should a vassal fail in his duty, or prove a traitor to his overlord, then the fief was forfeited, and the overlord took possession of it again—if he could.

The chief return which the overlord gave to his vassal for the military help and aids promised by his vassal was protection. And the rapid growth of the feudal system is due greatly to the need of this protection. In the lawless times which followed upon the break-up of Charlemagne's Empire the small landowners were at the mercy of the great. The land was full of marauding barons, and might was right. If a man was not strong enough to defend his life or his goods with his sword, another took it. It was easy enough for the baron, with twenty retainers at his back, to swoop down upon the poor knight who had but five, and having slain him, to take possession of all his goods and lands. So rather than lose both land and life, many of the lesser nobles who had held their lands in the old free way were glad to give them up to some powerful lord, and receive them again as fiefs together with the assurance of protection.

70

In theory the feudal system was an excellent way of maintaining an army for the benefit of the state with little expense to the state. If the king wished to go to war (and in those days he nearly always wished to go to war against one or other enemy) he called upon his great vassals to supply him with men. They called upon their vassals, they, in turn, upon theirs, and so on down the long line, until the lowest rank was reached, and a goodly company gathered to the royal standard.

In practice the results were by no means so good. In the first place, only the vassals-in-chief paid homage direct to the king. All other vassals paid homage and swore fealty to their own particular lord, duke, or count. The king was far off, he was but a name to many of his so-called subjects. The count or duke was near, he lived among his vassals; they knew him and, in fear or affection, followed him to battle wherever he led them, even against the king himself. In practice thus the great vassals were often stronger than the king, and when they rebelled against his authority he found it hard, or even impossible, to subdue them.

William the Conqueror and the Feudal System

The feudal system made a strong central government impossible, and the lands in which it flourished most became little more than a collection of independent and tumultuous states, each one of which was a miniature kingdom in itself.

In England this state of things was to a great extent avoided by the wisdom of William the Conqueror. He knew that as Duke of Normandy he was as strong, or stronger, in France than the king he owned as overlord. He determined that in England no vassal should be as strong as he. So in rewarding his Norman vassals by giving them English land, he was careful not to give any one of them a large tract in one place. If a vassal's deserts demanded a great reward he received not one large estate but several small ones scattered widely over the country. This made it difficult for a vassal to gather all his men-at-arms together without the fact coming to the king's knowledge. Besides this, William made all vassals swear fealty to himself direct, whether they received their land as vassals-in-chief or held it merely as sub-vassals from some duke or count.

Within his fief every feudal lord was absolute. He had the power of life and of death over his vassals. He was ruler and judge. He made war where and when he chose. For in those days private war was a common right. The pettiest baron might make war on his neighbour if he felt disposed, the only condition being that he must declare war with due ceremony before beginning to fight. This was done by sending a gage, generally a glove, to the enemy.

As war was a common right, every man rich enough not to require to work with his hands was a soldier. No other profession except that of a priest was open to a gentleman. Dignity did not allow the great lords to farm their own lands, and a life of idleness and a love of adventure drove them forth to fight on all and every occasion. So it came about that all the upper classes from the king to the poorest knight were soldiers. They were all gentlemen and idlers save for their profession as soldiers.

Beneath them, and sharply cut off from them, came the workers. They were divided into several classes, the lowest of which were villains and slaves. They were part and parcel with the land. When a fief passed from one overlord to another they passed with it. In life and in death they were tied to the land. They were as much their lord's property as his cattle, and could neither marry nor take any other great step in life without his permission.

Yet the villain was not a slave. He could not leave the land, it is true, but neither could his overlord take from him the small portion of land which had been granted to him, so long as he paid his dues. These dues generally consisted of a certain number of days' labour each year, and a certain proportion of his harvest and cattle. The slave, on the other hand, had no rights. He was absolutely in the hands of his overlord. He could be sold or even slain if his master so pleased.

TOURNAMENT AND FEUDAL WARFARE

BY the feudal system the world was divided into two great classes. The upper class was an aristocracy of soldiers, the lower class comprised all the workers. In both classes there were many grades, but between the richest peasant and the poorest squire there was a great gulf fixed which, in feudal times, it was almost impossible to cross.

Labour was the portion of the lower classes, war was both the profession and the amusement of the upper classes. And if by any chance there was no real war to occupy and amuse them, they played at it and got up mimic battles called tournaments.

These tournaments were generally fought in presence of the king or of some great noble and his ladies. Clad in full armour, as if for actual warfare, but armed with blunted weapons, the combatants rode at each other, each man trying not to kill but to unhorse his opponent. The knight who bore himself best, and brought the greatest number of opponents to the ground, was adjudged the winner, and received a prize.

But often tournaments were of a much more informal character. Indeed, for the youths of those times they took the place of the Saturday afternoon games of cricket or football of to-day. A writer of the twelfth century tells us that the young men of London were in the habit of holding a tournament every Sunday afternoon in Lent.

"A noble train of young men," he says, "take the field after dinner well mounted on horses of the best mettle. The citizens rush out of the gates in shoals, furnished with lances and shields, the younger sort with javelins, pointed, but disarmed of their steel. They ape the feats of war, and act the sham fight, practising the agonistic exercises of that kind. If the king happens to be near the city many courtiers honour them with their presence, together with the juvenile part of the households of the bishops, earls, and barons, such as are not yet dignified with the honour of knighthood, and are desirous of trying their skill. The hope of victory excites to emulation. The generous chargers neigh and champ the bit. At length when the course begins, and the youthful combatants are divided into classes or parties, one body retreats and another pursues, without being able to come up with them, whilst in another quarter the pursuers overtake the foe, unhorse them, and pass them, many a length."

But although tournaments were meant merely as trials of skill, they were often more deadly than real battles, and many a knight, who had passed unscathed through frequent wars, met his death in the lists.

For in the wars of the middle ages the nobles on opposing sides often tried, just as in tournaments, to unhorse and take prisoner their foes rather than slay them. This was not because of any tenderness to the foe, nor because of any desire to save life—for in those days the taking of life sat lightly on a man's conscience; it was merely a matter of business. War was the business of the nobles. It was necessary to make it pay. And although no noble would have stooped to work with his hands he was never averse to making a good bargain. For a living noble a large ransom could always be wrung out of the pockets of his vassals, while for his dead body they would pay nothing.

There was little that was ennobling or fine about these feudal wars. They were not uprisings against tyranny, they were not struggles for liberty, they were not patriotic. They were simply wars of aggression and greed. A man won possession of his land by his sword. And if by the sword he could not keep it, then another took it from him, and the weakest perished. It was the doctrine of the mailed fist.

Every great noble knew that he must be prepared to resist the attacks of his neighbour, for every neighbour was a possible enemy. So every castle became a fortress, built not for pleasure and beauty but for strength. Generally a high position, difficult of access and easy of defence, was chosen as a site. The buildings were defended by stone battlements of enormous strength and thickness, and surrounded by a moat crossed only by a drawbridge which could be raised at pleasure from within. So strong were they that before gunpowder was invented it was almost impossible to take them except by starving the defenders. In feudal wars, therefore, sieges bulk largely.

Feudal Estates of the Clergy

Many of the abbeys and monasteries, too, were fortresses. Like Durham they were "Half house of God, half castle 'gainst the Scot" or other enemy. The great among the clergy were also great feudal lords, and they were just as eager to increase the domains of their abbeys and monasteries as were the secular lords to add to their manors and estates. We hear of a bishop, who, "not content with the dignity of his office, next anticipated in his mind how he might accomplish great and wonderful things. For he possessed a haughty speaking mouth, with the proudest heart. At last, having collected a band of needy and desperate men, he began his mad career, and became, like Nimrod, a mighty hunter before the Lord, forgetting that his office required him to be, with Peter, a fisher of men. Every day he was joined by troops of adherents, among whom he was conspicuous above all by the head and shoulders, and like some mighty commander he inflamed their desires."

For a time he was successful in all his undertakings, and became an object of terror even to the king; but at length he met his match in another bishop, "a man of singular simplicity" who, when tribute was demanded of him, refused, and went forth to do battle against his marauding brother-bishop. "And by God's grace he threw a hatchet which felled his enemy to the earth as he rode in the van."

At another time we hear of an abbot who rode to the siege of Windsor, "where he appeared in arms with some other abbots of England, and had his own standard. He had there also many knights at great expense." But, says his biographer, "we who were cloistered monks considered this course of action to be fraught with danger, fearing lest some future abbot might be compelled to go to war in person."

The Truce of God

But although there were many warlike churchmen, there were far more who saw, with grief, the awful devastation made by the constant wars between the nobles. At length, through their influence, the Truce of God was announced. By this Truce fighting was forbidden from Wednesday evening till Monday morning, so that the days upon which Christ suffered, died, and rose again should, at least, be kept free from strife. Besides this, war was forbidden altogether during Lent and Advent, and upon all great feasts and vigils. Thus, if the Truce of God had been fully enforced, only about a quarter of the year remained in which it was lawful to fight. This was, however, far too short a time for the turbulent nobles, and the Truce was many times broken. Yet the Church was so powerful that it often found means to punish those who broke the Truce, and bring them to submission.

That the Church was able to pronounce the Truce of God at all shows how powerful it had become. It was the duty of kings to keep peace within their dominions. But they were unable to do it. So the Church stepped in and performed the duty for them, and the Truce of God remained more or less in force until the thirteenth century. Then the power of the rulers increased, and in time the "King's Peace" took the place of that of the Church.

THE HOLY ROMAN EMPIRE—
SAXON EMPERORS

THE fortunes of the three countries carved out of the Empire of Charlemagne were widely different. France slowly, but surely, became welded into a nation, but Germany remained merely a conglomeration of independent states. For while France struggled towards unity, Germany chased after the phantom of world dominion, claiming with the title of emperor the right to rule over Italy. This claim brought great evil to Italy, it brought scarcely less evil to Germany. It produced endless wars and strife with the Church, it was a constant hindrance to the real progress of Germany, and for nine hundred years it prevented Italy from becoming a united nation.

Feebleness of Later Carolingians

The family of Charlemagne died out in feebleness. Of that feebleness we get some idea from the names borne by the last rulers of his house, such as "the Bald," "the Fat," "the Simple," "the Child." In Germany the line came to an end in 911 with Louis the Child; in France it lasted a little longer, and came to an end in 987 with Louis the Fainéant. In both countries upon the death of the last Carolingian the nobles met together and chose a successor from among their number. But whereas in France the monarchy at once became hereditary, and remained so until the Revolution, in Germany an elective monarchy continued, in name at least, until the eighteenth century.

Upon the death of Louis the Child the German nobles chose Conrad of Franconia as their ruler. But his power was visionary. The great princes ruled like kings in their own domains, quarrelling among themselves and flouting imperial authority.

Still, small although his power was, Conrad kept the Empire from being broken up into absolutely independent states. He saw, however, how slight his influence was, and at his death he prayed the princes to choose as his successor, not one of his own family, but Henry of Saxony.

The Saxon Emperors

The nobles followed Conrad's advice, and Henry became the first of the Saxon emperors who held the regal power in Germany for more than a hundred years, 918-1024. For although the crown was elective in theory, it very often descended from father to son, the son being chosen and crowned as successor in his father's lifetime.

Conrad kept the Empire from falling asunder. Henry gave it some sort of unity, the effect of which lasted long after his death. He wrought peace within the Empire, forcing the great princes to own him as overlord, so that before the end of his reign there was no German-speaking people who did not own allegiance to the Empire. He quelled the fierce Hungarians who were a constant menace to the German states. He built towns, encouraged industries and agriculture, and colonized many parts of Germany which had before been almost bare of inhabitants.

Henry gave his life to Germany, and did not trouble about Italy, or the phantom glory of the imperial title, and therein lay much of his success. Towards the end of his life, indeed, when his work for Germany seemed done, he felt the fatal lure, and made up his mind to go to Rome to be crowned. But he died before his purpose was accomplished.

Henry was succeeded by his son Otto I, the Great. He was only twenty-four when he came to the throne, and the powerful nobles who had bowed to his father refused to bow to him. So his reign began with civil war, the chief among the rebels being members of his own family. His reign, indeed, was full of wars at home and abroad, but in the end he was victorious everywhere. He subjugated the Bohemians, he forced the Danes to own him as overlord, and in the great battle of Lechfield in 955, he so thoroughly defeated the Hungarians that they ceased to be a menace to Germany, and began to settle down in a civilized manner in the country which is still called by their name.

Otto I—Dreams of World Dominion

By all these wars Otto strengthened and consolidated his kingdom, and Germany took a first place among the states of Europe. But unfortunately for the future of Germany Otto's ambition did not end there. Germany was not everything to him as it had been to his father. His thoughts turned to world dominion, and when the Princess Adelheid of Italy prayed him to come and release her from the oppression of King Berenger, he answered her call eagerly.

Otto defeated Berenger, married the Princess Adelheid, and took the

78

title of king of Italy. Then he marched to Rome and received the imperial crown at the hands of the pope.

For more than sixty years no German king had held the title of emperor, and during that time Germany had made strides towards unity. The title meanwhile had not lapsed, but it had been held by petty kings, who had little power and who were of no account in the politics of Europe. In theory the holder was the secular lord of the world, in theory he was overlord of every king or prince in Europe, but having been held by princes of no real power, men had grown to regard it little. Now Otto, already a great and powerful ruler, pulled the imperial title out of the mud, and made it great again. From his reign, in fact, we may date the true beginning of the Holy Roman Empire. He revived the Empire of Charlemagne, with less territory indeed, but with no less splendour. But in doing this he linked the fortunes of Germany with those of Italy, to the lasting misfortune of both. To both the connection was fatal. Instead of strengthening their own kingdom, henceforth the German kings, driven on by the baleful enchantment, dreamt of world-power, and for nine hundred years poured out blood and treasure in a vain endeavour to subjugate Italy, thus keeping Germany weak and Italy disunited.

Meanwhile Otto ruled the Empire with a high hand. He even ruled the Church, for by the middle of the tenth century the papacy had fallen low, and the lives of the popes had become a scandal. Otto dethroned popes at will and imposed others of his own choosing on the Roman people, and so asserted his power that by the end of his reign he had pulled the papacy, even as he had pulled the imperial title, out of the mud in which he had found it. But the Church was under the state; the popes had to bow to the emperor's will.

THE HOLY ROMAN EMPIRE—THE STRUGGLE
BETWEEN POPE AND EMPEROR

THREE Saxon Emperors followed Otto. Then, with Henry II the line came to an end, and with Conrad II that of the Franconian emperors began, and lasted for a hundred years. With the second of these emperors, Henry III, the Empire reached the height of its power, and appeared more like a united whole than ever before. For Henry was one of the best and strongest rulers of the middle ages.

In nothing, perhaps, did Henry show himself greater than in curbing private war in Germany. In neighbouring states the Truce of God had been proclaimed. Henry imposed upon his people the King's Peace. In this peace the land prospered as it had never done before. Peasants tilled their fields in safety, and merchants passed from town to town unmolested.

Henry III and the Papacy

In the Church, too, Henry made his power felt. The papacy had again sunk into the slough from which Otto I had drawn it, and three popes struggled for the papal throne. Henry deposed all three and installed as pope a German, a member of the imperial house. Indeed, during his reign he installed no fewer than four popes, all of them Germans. Under them the papacy was raised from its degraded position. But in thus helping to purify and, in consequence, strengthen the Church, Henry, all unconsciously, laid the foundations of the great struggle between the Empire and the papacy. For the time, however, the Emperor's triumph over the Church was complete, and it seemed as if imperial supremacy was firmly and enduringly fixed.

But in thus giving his time and thought to things papal and Italian, Henry lost much of his influence in Germany, and in the last years of his life troubles gathered thick about him. In the midst of these he died, leaving a child of six to succeed him.

With a child upon the throne the bands by which Henry III had bound the Empire together loosened. The power of the emperor became less, the power of the princes became far greater than it had ever been

80

since the time of Otto I. The princes rose against the emperor, they fought among themselves, and the whole land was filled with strife.

Henry IV and Gregory VII

It was when the Empire was thus weakened that the monk Hildebrand, who had already become a great power in the Church was elected as pope. He chose the name of Gregory VII, and under that name he became even more powerful than he had been as Hildebrand. Between him and Henry IV a bitter struggle for supremacy began.

Two years after his inauguration Gregory issued a decree declaring that henceforth bishops should not be chosen by the emperor nor by any lay person, but that the investiture should be entirely in the hands of the Church. Now emperor after emperor had tried to strengthen the clergy in order to curb the power of the nobles. And to do this emperor after emperor had given them lands to hold in fief, until at length a great part of the soil of Germany was in their hands. If, then, the pope alone had power to appoint bishops, all these lands would pass into his control, and the imperial authority would be seriously lessened.

Henry was at this time only twenty-five. He was passionate and ill-balanced, and little calculated to cope with a pope of overweening pride and terrible severity. He was in no mood to yield up any of his authority, and he deposed the pope. For had not his father elected and deposed popes as he would. But Gregory was no German pope, ready to bow to the commands of a German king. Instead of being cowed by this show of imperial power, he replied to it by excommunicating Henry and threatening to depose him if he remained impenitent.

Never before had a pope dared to use such arrogance towards an emperor, and had Henry been surrounded by faithful vassals, had he ruled over a united people, the thunders of the pope might have fallen harmless upon him; but because of that dream of world dominion Germany was not united. There was little German loyalty to a ruler who claimed the world as his dominion. Every prince of the Empire was constantly seeking an opportunity to become an independent ruler. Now many saw their opportunity, for the pope had set them free from their allegiance, and Henry found his empire filled with rebellion and his authority vanishing into thin air.

Henry soon saw that only by submitting to the pope could he regain his authority over his rebellious subjects, and he made up his mind to submit at once. It was no repentance for his deed which urged him to this, but merely political necessity. In midwinter he crossed the Alps, and after incredible hardships reached Canossa, where the haughty pope awaited him. There, one bitter winter morning, while the snow lay on the ground, the proud emperor appeared before the castle gates of the still prouder pope. Clad in the garb of a penitent, with head and feet bare, he humbly knocked, begging admission. But the door remained closed. A second and a third day passed, and still Henry stood without the gates, waiting the pleasure of the stern old man within.

At length Gregory relented. The penitent king was admitted to his presence, and received absolution. Thus did the inexorable priest uphold before the eyes of all Christendom the papal right to judge kings. Thus did he make good his claim to loose and to bind in earthly as in heavenly Matters, "to give and to take away empires, kingdoms, princedoms, and the possessions of all men." Without striking a blow, without even having an army behind him, this little, grey-haired priest had conquered "the lord of the world."

But the pope, by his haughty measures, had made an implacable enemy of Henry, and as soon as he felt himself strong enough he defied the pope anew. Again he was excommunicated, and again he replied by deposing the pope. This time he set up an anti-pope and marching to Rome beseiged Gregory there.

After a siege of three years Henry entered the city and received the imperial crown at the hands of his own pope, Clement III. Gregory's day was over, and he fled to Salerno. There he died, but even in death he did not forgive the recreant emperor, and he died leaving his enemy still under the ban of the Church.

Rebellion and civil war filled Henry's last days, and at length, deposed, betrayed, and beggared, he died. But the pope's curse followed him even beyond the grave, and not until five years later was the ban removed and the bones of Henry IV laid to rest in consecrated ground.

Concordat of Worms

Gregory VII was dead, Henry IV was dead, but the struggle over the investiture continued. For succeeding popes clung to the great powers

Gregory had claimed, succeeding emperors resisted them. Henry V succeeded his father, Henry IV. He had rebelled against his father during his lifetime, and now the new pope, Paschal II, hoped to find in him an obedient servant; but he was mistaken, and the struggle continued. At length, however, at the Concordat of Worms, Calixtus II being now pope, an agreement was come to. It was agreed that the pope should have the right to investiture with ring and crozier, but that bishops should be chosen with the consent of the emperor, and that they should do homage to him for their fiefs in the same way as laymen.

Thus the struggle of fifty years ended. The pope was, in the main, victorious, for although he had not been able to make good all his claims, he had won much prestige, whereas the emperor had lost much. But although the question of investiture might be settled, the rivalry between pope and emperor, each arrogantly claiming to rule the world, continued as before. More and more the popes strove to make good their claim to be not only the chief priests but the chief princes of Christendom. But it is not uninteresting to note the difference in the treatment meted out by them to Henry of Germany and William of England.

In England the king was supreme in Church and state. There the people alone could give or take away the crown, there the king made and unmade bishops without reference to the pope. But in the hope of making England a fief of the Church the pope, Alexander II, blessed the enterprise of William of Normandy when he set forth to conquer the kingdom from Harold the Saxon. William, however, pious Churchman as he was, having conquered England, meant to rule there as sole master. Gregory VII also meant to rule there as elsewhere, and after some preliminary skirmishes in which William yielded nothing, he sent a messenger to demand from the king of England an oath probably of fealty, together with the assurance that Peter's Pence should be more punctually paid.

William's reply was very short, very decisive. Bluntly he refused to own himself the pope's man. The kings of England who had gone before him had never sworn fealty to the pope; neither would he. As to Peter's Pence, from ancient times it had been paid, and he would continue to pay it. What was lawfully due to the pope the pope should have. The respect due to the chief priest of Christendom he should also have, and nothing more. The right of investiture, over which pope and emperor quarrelled so fiercely, was never even mentioned, and whatever wrath Gregory may have felt at William's refusal of fealty, no thunders of the Church were launched at the recreant king. This was partly, doubtless, because Gregory was otherwise occupied. His arch-enemy the emperor was again defiant, and had enthroned an anti-pope, and Gregory, gathering his forces to combat him, had little leisure to fight the king of England.

But if the popes were unsuccessful in pressing their claims in England, in Germany they were more successful. During the reign of Lothaire the Saxon, who followed Henry V as ruler of Germany, their power increased. For Lothaire was weakly fearful of arousing the pope's wrath, and he even went so far as to acknowledge the pope as his overlord, in respect of some Italian lands, of which he might have claimed possession outright.

THE PROGRESS OF FRANCE TOWARDS NATIONALITY

The Capetians

FOR more than a century after the Treaty of Verdun (see Chapter X) the Carolingian dynasty struggled on in France and at length, with Louis the Fainéant, it died out in feebleness.

The first king of the new dynasty was Hugh Capet, Count of Paris, and from him the dynasty is known as that of the Capetians. They ruled in France for nearly three and a half centuries.

Hugh Capet came to the throne of France not by inheritance but by election, and in spite of his title as king, he had little more power than he had had as count. His so-called vassals, the dukes of Normandy and Burgundy, the Counts of Anjou, Flanders, and Champagne, might do homage indeed for their lands, but they ruled over these lands like independent sovereigns, paying little or no heed to the wishes or commands of their overlord the king.

There was no awe or reverence for the king's majesty. If, in theory, by his grace they enjoyed the title of duke or count he, no less by their grace, enjoyed that of king. And the angry question which Hugh addressed to one of these turbulent nobles, "Who made you count?" merely brought forth the sharp retort, "Who made you king?"

But weak although it was at first, the Capetian dynasty persisted. King followed king upon the throne without question or revolt. And this fact alone gave at length to the government a stability quite unknown to the neighbouring feudal state of Germany.

William the Conqueror

The chief event of European importance during the reigns of the first Capetians was the conquest of England by William, Duke of Normandy, in the reign of Philip I. By becoming king of England William became a far more powerful sovereign than his overlord the king of France, and the conquest of England by him had almost as great consequences for France as for England. For it laid the foundation of the English king's claim to French land, a claim which plunged both countries into war for hundreds of years. It was during the reign of Philip I's son, Louis VI, that the long struggle between English and French for supremacy in France began. Louis VI was the first king of France to make his power truly felt. As a young man he was known as Louis the Fighter, or Louis the Wide-awake, and he spent the first years of his reign in subjugating the turbulent princes of the realm. He fought them, imprisoned them, and threw down their great castles where they had lived in freedom, oppressing whom they would. And in the end he forced many of them to recognize the superior authority of the king, and to respect the King's Peace and the King's Justice.

But while quelling the nobles Louis protected the villains and the serfs. It was with their help, indeed, that Louis subdued the nobles, and in return for that help he frequently granted them charters of freedom. Thus, from being slaves they became free men. They built towns and surrounded them with walls like the castles of the nobles, coming and going at will, working for whom they would, no longer being tied to the land and forced to serve their overlord. Thus the citizen or burgher class began to rise in France.

The prince whom Louis VI found hardest to subdue was Henry I, king of England who, as duke of Normandy, was Louis's vassal. For Henry had the resources of a kingdom behind him, and when he rebelled against his overlord it was much more than the rebellion of a mere vassal. It was an invasion by a foreign king and the introduction of a foreign influence.

Louis's task was therefore twofold. He endeavoured, first, to subdue the feudal power to the regal power; secondly, he endeavoured to oust foreign influence and unify and nationalize his whole kingdom. These two endeavours form the groundwork of French history for hundreds of years.

Henry II's Angevin Kingdom

Louis VI was, to some extent, successful in keeping his great vassal of England in check, but under his son Louis VII that vassal again became more powerful. For Louis VII made the great mistake of allowing Henry, Count of Anjou and Duke of Normandy, to marry his own divorced wife, Eleanor of Aquitaine. By this marriage Henry became lord of the whole south-west of France which, added to Normandy, Anjou, and Maine, made him ruler of a domain larger than that of the French king.

Two years after his marriage with Eleanor Henry became king of England. Thus strengthened, he began to dream of establishing a great Angevin Empire which would include the whole of France and England. But Henry II's ambitions were frustrated partly through the rebellion of his own sons.

Philip Augustus

Louis VII died in 1180 and was succeeded by his able, brave, if not too scrupulous son, Philip Augustus. France for Frenchmen might have been his motto. It was certainly his aim, and to advance it he made use of the quarrels between Henry II and his sons, siding with these sons and making a great friend of Richard. But when Henry II died, and Philip's one-time friend Richard became king of England, Philip fought him as he had fought his father Henry. He made, however, little headway against the superior military genius of the English king, and it was not until the infamous John Lackland came to the throne of England that the French king's moment arrived.

With the advent of John the struggle entered on a new phase, and the end could not long be doubtful. For on the one side there was an indolent, vicious king, barely tolerated by an alienated people. On the other there was an energetic, calculating soldier-statesman, with behind him a people in whom the sense of loyalty and of nationality was fast awakening.

Every advantage that was his Philip used with vigour. One by one he wrested his French possessions from the English king, until there was nothing left to him except Gascony. John, overwhelmed with troubles at home, fighting his own barons, and casting defiance at the pope, let his French possessions slip from him. But when he saw them gone he desired to have them back again. So he made an alliance with Otto IV, emperor of Germany, and together they made an attack on France. While John landed in the south-west the emperor invaded the north-east. But Philip had little fear of John. He left his son Louis to deal with him, and himself marched against the German emperor.

Battle of Bouvines

The two forces met at Bouvines, a few miles from Lille, and here one of the great decisive battles of the Middle Ages was fought. The emperor and his allies were utterly defeated. Otto, barely escaping with his life, fled back to Germany, to find himself disowned and rejected, while Philip returned in triumph to Paris, where the people greeted him with cheers and cast flowers in his path. Henceforth he was no longer merely the overlord of French barons, he was king of the French people. The national spirit was awake.

Philip's wars against John of England had brought him broad and fair lands, and had made him the greatest feudal overlord in France. By the battle of Bouvines, and his defeat of the German emperor he won not an inch of territory but he gained for France a first place among the nations of Europe. For from the thirteenth century France takes a leading place. England was still only England, not the United Kingdom, and the great Colonial Empire still undreamed of; Germany, pursuing the quest for world dominion, had already fallen from the high place won for it by Otto and by Henry III. Italy and Spain were without union or nationality; Russia had not yet taken its place as a European nation.

KNIGHTHOOD

THE Middle Ages was a time of unrestrained lawlessness and greed. Yet out of this time there grew something fine in the ideas of chivalry and the orders of knighthood. We cannot tell when the idea of chivalry began, any more than we can say when feudalism began. It grew up out of the needs of the time.

The word chivalry is of French origin, coming from cheval, a horse, and chevalier, a horseman; and it was in France, perhaps, that chivalry found its truest home. As the nobles and gentlemen were the only horsemen of feudal times, it was with them alone that chivalry had to do. In time it entered into everything connected with the life of the nobles, softening to some extent the brutality of it, casting a glamour of romance over their deeds, and giving them a religious enthusiasm.

Those who entered the orders of chivalry were called knights. The word comes from the Anglo-Saxon cniht, and originally meant boy or youth. All knights were made, not born. A man might be born a prince, but he could only become a knight after long years of probation and training.

This training began as a rule when the boy was seven years old. He was then sent to the castle of some friendly lord where he became a page. He waited on his lady in her bower, and stood behind his master's chair in hall, learning the dignity of obedience and the beauty of gentleness. He was also trained in every knightly exercise, learning how to use sword and spear, to ride, and to fly a falcon. Thus every feudal castle became a school where a boy might learn everything which, in those days, it was thought necessary for a gentleman to know.

When about the age of fifteen the page became a squire. As squire he still had to perform many household and personal duties, such as carving at table, presenting the wine-cup to his master or chief guests, or attending upon his lady when she rode abroad. But more and more of his time was taken up with knightly exercises, and he learned to wear armour, to ride a war horse, and take part in tournaments. In time of war, too, he now rode forth with his master in battle, bore his shield, and helped him to don his armour.

Besides all this the knight-aspirant, both as page and squire, was taught to reverence ladies, and to be courteous and gentle in his behaviour towards them. This showed a wonderful advance in civilization. For women were in those days of small account. They were looked upon as little more than possessions. They were weak, and therefore, under the rule of the mailed fist, might be taken advantage of. The laws of chivalry taught men to protect them and to fight for them if need be.

Having for five or six years proved himself faithful in all his duties, and fearless in the face of danger, the squire received the honour of knighthood. This was conferred upon him with solemn ceremony.

First of all a bath was taken with great formality. This was a sort of new baptism, a symbol that past sins were washed away. Then the knight-aspirant was clad in a white robe, the token of purity, over it was placed a red robe to signify the blood which he would have to shed in fulfilment of the vows he was about to take, and lastly, over all, a black cloak was thrown as a reminder that death would come to him as to all men.

Thus purified and clothed anew the squire was led to the Church. It was evening now, and the building was filled with dim, mysterious shadows, and here, before the altar, he was left alone to watch the long night through. This was called the vigil of arms. To sit down was forbidden to the aspirant, so standing or kneeling before the altar he spent the silent, lonely hours of darkness in prayer and thought.

When day dawned the silence was broken by the coming of the priests. Mass was said, the squire confessed, and receiving absolution, partook of the sacrament. Then, in the presence of a joyous company, consisting of all the ladies, knights, squires, and pages which went to make up the household of a great noble, the most solemn part of the ceremony took place.

First the squire was fully clad in armour. The most noble and gentle knights present bound on his spurs and signed his knees with the sign of the cross. Then his sword, after being blessed by the priest, was girded on. At length, fully clad in all the panoply of war, the squire knelt before the priest, vowing faithfully to serve the Church and the king, to shun no adventure of his person in any good cause, to protect widows and orphans, and women distressed or abandoned, to serve his ladylove in faith and honour, to be courteous and truthful, and, above all things else, to die a thousand deaths rather than break his word or deny his religion.

These vows being taken, the squire was next led to the noble about to confer knighthood upon him, and again kneeling, he received on his neck a resounding blow from the flat of his sword. This was the accolade. "Be brave knight," said the noble; or, "May God and St. George make thee good knight," and the ceremony was over.

Then, springing up, the new knight leapt upon his waiting charger without touching the stirrup, and, lance in hand, rode off to demolish before an admiring crowd the dummy foes set up for the purpose. This being done, the rest of the day was spent in feasting and rejoicing.

It was only by degrees that so much ceremony gathered about the making of a knight. At first it was a much simpler matter, consisting of little more than the accolade. It was only by degrees, too, that it took on its religious character, for at first it was purely military.

As the ceremony and splendour of the occasion increased so did the cost. The fitting out of a new knight alone was costly, including as it did robes, armour, arms, horses, falcons, and many other things which were deemed necessary for the equipment of a noble. Besides this, money was distributed among the poor, rich presents were given to the minstrels who attended at the ceremony, new robes and furs were provided for the ladies of the household and often for the guests.

Knights Errant

For this reason, as you remember, the knighting of his eldest son was one of the occasions upon which an overlord had the right to call for an "aid" in money from his vassals. For this reason, too, many a poor gentleman in spite of great and valiant deeds, which would have entitled him to become a knight, remained a squire all his life, not having the wherewithal to pay the expenses of being knighted.

There was, however, another mode in which knighthood was conferred. This was on the battle-field. Here there was no expense and no ceremony save the accolade. Any knight of renown could make a knight, and the squire had but to kneel before him and receive the accolade. Knighthood was thus conferred after a battle as a reward for bravery. But it was just as frequently conferred before a battle as an incitement to brave deeds. Indeed, there was hardly a battle in the Middle Ages when no new knights were made either before or after.

In this way many poor gentlemen who had no other fortune but their swords became knights. Having neither home nor land they wandered about the world seeking occasions upon which to show their prowess, and so win fame and at the same time wealth. These became known as knights errant, and they figure largely in the Romances of the time.

An errant knight
Well horsed, and large of limb, Sir Gaudwin hight,
He, nor of castle nor of land was lord,
Houseless he reaped the harvest of his sword.
And now, not more on fame than profit bent,
Rode with blithe heart unto the tournament.

The knight errant was ready to fight for any cause however mad, so long as honour and loyalty did not forbid. For with the coming of chivalry there arose ideas of honour, faith, and courtesy, and any knight who transgressed against these ideas was liable to degradation—many did, as a matter of fact so transgress, and go unpunished—but retribution sometimes overtook him.

Then he was put to shame, and cast out of the brotherhood of arms, with ceremony as solemn as that of his initiation.

By the most noble knights of the district the recreant was clad in full armour, as if about to take the field. Then he was led to the church, where a high stage had been erected upon which he was made to mount. There thirteen priests said the prayers and psalms used for the dead, and at the end of each prayer one piece of his armour was taken from him and cast upon the ground.

As each piece was so cast down the heralds cried aloud the reason for its removal. "This is the helmet of a disloyal and miscreant knight!" they cried; "we cast it away, for it has sheltered traitorous eyes." Or again, "We take thy gauntlet, for it has covered a corrupt hand," and so with each piece. Then the knight's sword was broken over his head, his spurs were hacked from his heels, and at last he stood before the eyes of the whole congregation, bare of all arms and armour.

After this a basin of gold or silver full of water was brought, and the heralds cried aloud, "What is this knight's name?"

The pursuivants answered, giving his real name, whereupon the king-at-arms replied, "That is not true. For he is a miscreant and false traitor and one who has broken the ordinance of knighthood."

The priests then spoke. "Let us give him his right name," they said. And the heralds sounded their trumpets and cried aloud, "What shall be done with him?"

Then the king replied. "Let him be with dishonour and shame banished from my kingdom as a vile and infamous man that hath done offence against the honour of knighthood." When the king had spoken the heralds cast the water on the degraded knight's face, as though he were baptized anew, and cried, "Henceforth thou shalt be called by thy right name—Traitor."

Then the king, with twelve knights, put on mourning garments in token of sorrow, and coming to the degraded knight they put a rope round his neck, and threw him from the stage, not by the steps by which he had honourably climbed up but over the edge. Finally, with every imaginable insult and ignominy he was led to the altar. There, while he lay groveling on the ground a Psalm full of curses was read over him. Then all men turned from him, and left him for ever alone with his misery and degradation.

Thus were the unworthy thrust out from the great and noble brotherhood of knights.

In days when books were few, when few gentlemen even outside the monasteries could read or write, when therefore they had little occupation for their minds, and when occupation for their hands was denied them, the effects of the training of chivalry on the manhood of the times was great. It taught them, if fight they must, to fight for something more than mere lust of blood and plunder. It held before them great ideals, and if few attained to them, many were at least lifted above the brutal slough of utter selfishness.

With the Truce of God the Church tried to curb the fighting instinct of the feudal lords: with chivalry it tried to consecrate it. The latter was less difficult and more successful. Under the influence of the chivalric ideals western Europe became flooded with a soldier aristocracy, embued with a passionate devotion for the Church, overflowing with a romantic and sublime enthusiasm seeking some adequate outlet. This outlet the Church also was to supply.

THE BEGINNING OF THE CRUSADES

Pilgrimages to the Holy Land

WE to whom the story of Christ has been familiar from earliest childhood can hardly realize with what force that story struck upon the hearts of the heathen peoples of Europe when first they heard it. They were fierce and savage men given over to war and bloodshed. And when they were told of the gentle Christ who not only loved his fellows but gave his life for them, their simple savage hearts were filled with amazement and adoration. With their wonder there grew up an intense desire to see for themselves the spot on earth where that marvellous story had been unfolded. So great grew that desire that in spite of all difficulties and dangers many set out to visit the Holy Land. Even in very early times, from the islands of the sea, from the forests of Germany, from the scattered villages of France, from the mountains of Italy, from every corner of Europe which Christian teachers had reached, pilgrims set forth.

To-day the journey is easy, safe, and rapid. Then it was slow, difficult, and dangerous. To-day the journey is an affair of days. Then it was one of months and even years, and a man who set forth on a pilgrimage to Jerusalem said farewell to his dear ones as to those he might never see again. Many never returned: and some, indeed, set forth in such passionate exaltation that they prayed God to grant them the blessing of death in the holy place.

Those who did return brought with them a kind of halo of saintship. Their friends regarded them with veneration, for their feet had trodden the paths over which Christ Himself had passed, they had knelt at the Holy Sepulchre and stood upon the Mount of Olives. It seemed as if something of holiness must cling even to their garments, and pilgrims kept carefully the clothes they had worn on entering into Jerusalem, so that they might be buried in them.

In time a pilgrimage to the Holy Land became a sort of act of grace, and the mere going there made a man clean of his sins however black they had been. So year by year the stream of pilgrims increased. Kings and emperors, princes and princessess, joined the throng. Splendid Christian churches were built in Jerusalem, a Patriarch or chief bishop of Jerusalem was appointed, and many Christians took up their abode there.

While Palestine still formed part of the Eastern Empire pilgrims came and went in peace. But in 637 it was conquered by the Mohammedans. This, however, hardly checked the flow of pilgrims to the Holy City. For to the Mohammedan Christ was a prophet, one less great indeed than Mohammed, but still a prophet. The Christians were, it is true, forbidden to build any more churches, were ordered to remove the crosses from those already built, and to cease the ringing of bells. They were forbidden also to carry weapons or ride on horses, and were forced to wear a distinctive dress. Otherwise they were left in peace to worship as they chose.

So for more than three hundred and fifty years under Moslim rule Christian pilgrims still thronged to Palestine. There were, of course, constant dangers from robbers and other evil-doers by the way. At times, too, there were sudden waves of persecution and oppression, but for the most part pilgrims came and went in peace.

Captured by the Turks

At length, however, in the first half of the eleventh century a new and terrible enemy appeared. These were the Turks. Like so many other invaders of Europe the Turks came from the East. They were fierce and cruel, and being converted to Mohammedanism they were filled with a savage zeal for their faith. In conquering hordes they swept through Persia and enthroned one of their leaders as king. Soon Palestine also fell before them, and the streets of Jerusalem flowed red with the blood of Christians. The holy places were profaned, the most solemn sacraments of the Church were made a cause of scornful laughter, while the aged Patriarch was dragged through the streets by the hair of his head, and cast into a loathsome dungeon, there to languish until a heavy ransom should be paid for his release.

The Christians who escaped death or imprisonment fled back to Europe. Here they spread abroad the tale of woe and desecration until all Europe wa,s shaken with wrath against the infidel.

Peter the Hermit and Urban II

Among those who returned was a pilgrim named Peter the Hermit.

Much of the story of Peter the Hermit is now looked upon as mere legend. It has even been said that he never visited Jerusalem at all. But whether that is so or not he undoubtedly helped to preach the first Crusade. He was a thin and wiry little man, and utterly insignificant save for his eyes, which burned with an almost mad enthusiasm. He had, too, a marvellous power of speech. And as he passed through Europe riding upon an ass, clad in a rough hair shirt, his head and feet bare, and carrying a crucifix in his hand, people flocked to hear him.

And wherever he spoke men felt their hearts uplifted by his glowing words, felt themselves impelled to fight in the name of God. They soon looked upon him as a saint, and were happy if they might touch his robe or even the ass upon which he rode. So from place to place they followed him, hanging on his words, weeping at the pictures which he drew of the miseries endured by the faithful.

But alone Peter could have done little. A poor priest might indeed arouse the enthusiasm of the people. It needed a greater power than his to direct that enthusiasm. That greater power was ready to hand.

The Eastern Empire had long been in a state of feebleness and decay. Now the emperor, Alexius Comnenus, saw with dismay territory after territory being reft from him by the infidel Turks, whose standards were planted almost within sight of the towers of Constantinople. Of himself he knew not how to stay their conquering march, so he sent messengers to the pope, Urban II, begging him for help.

The pope was not unwilling to listen to him, for he, too, was eager to drive the Turks back to their Asian deserts, and free the Holy Land from their oppression. So he called the people together to a conference at Piacenza in Italy. But although an immense crowd gathered to listen to him no decision was come to. It was not in Italy but in France, the true son of the Church, that the first action was to be taken; and crossing the Alps the pope held another conference at Clermont.

Conference of Clermont

Here such an immense crowd gathered that no room could be found for them in the town, and winter though it was, a vast city of tents sprang up all around. No building was large enough to contain the vast assemblage, and the conference was held in the open air. The pope, clad in

97

gorgeous robes, and surrounded by his cardinals, sat upon a throne erected in the market-place. And when he rose to speak deep silence fell upon the gathered thousands. Urban was a Frenchman, and he spoke not in Latin, the language of the learned and the Church, but in French, so that even the humblest who heard him could understand.

As the burning words of the great pontiff fell upon their ears the people wept and cried aloud, and their hearts glowed within them. Urban pictured to them the fury and the pride of the infidel, he reminded them of the great and glorious deeds of Charles the Hammer and of Charlemagne, and bade them go forth as they did against the foe. He bade them cease from warring against each other, and turn their swords upon the despoilers of the holy places.

"Let all hatred depart from among you," he cried. "Let your strife cease, let war be no more. Enter upon the path which leads to the Holy Sepulchre, wrest the land from the people of sin, and make it your own. For this spot the Saviour of mankind has made glorious by His birth, has made beautiful by His life, has made holy by His passion and redeemed by His death. Take, therefore, this journey eagerly for the remission of your sins, sure of the reward of eternal glory in the kingdom of heaven."

And when the pope had ceased speaking all the people cried out, "God wills it! God wills it!"

Then with frenzied eagerness they crowded round the pope to receive at his hands the cross which was to be their badge as soldiers of Christ. From this badge the expeditions which, during nearly two hundred years, were to change the face of Europe took their name of Crusades. A new word was thus given to language, and now any enthusiastic campaign against evil we call a crusade.

With the Crusades something new was brought into the idea of war. First, there was the idea of God. For every man who took the cross felt that he had enlisted under the banner of God Himself. Secondly, there was the idea of combat for a noble and unselfish end. Hitherto men had waged war for selfish ends and personal gain. But the Crusader sallied forth not to add broad acres to his land but to fight for the honour of God, and that the poor and unarmed pilgrim might visit the Holy Land in safety and peace. Thirdly, there was an element of freedom introduced. For the Crusader went forth, not at the command of his overlord to fight because he was bound by oath to follow his lord when he called—he went of his own will, to fight in a cause of his own choosing.

There were, of course, many who did not take the cross in this spirit of sacrifice or devotion. Some went merely for the love of adventure, some in the hope of enriching themselves through plunder or trade. Others, with few or no lands at home, went in the hope of founding principalities abroad. Criminals went to escape justice, debtors to escape payment of their debts, for the pope announced that every man who took the cross was free of his debts until his return. But although the reasons which men had for taking the cross were many and varied, the moving spirit, the one which overbalanced all others, was one of religious devotion and sacrifice.

Never before had a war been undertaken by the people of Europe in such a spirit. Chivalry, it is true, had already given to knighthood something of a holy character, and had set before the true knight ideals other than those of mere plunder and bloodshed. But even so the influence of religion had been but little felt amidst the violence and bloodshed of feudal wars. Even the romantic knight errant had fought for gain, and had been willing to sell his sword to the highest bidder.

The Early Crusades

The Crusaders did not constitute an army in our sense of the word. They were merely a conglomeration of armed and unarmed bands who travelled together towards the Holy Land. They were drawn from every country of western Europe, but for no country was the first Crusade a national enterprise. Many Frenchmen it is true joined the expedition, for these romantic adventures appealed to the French more than to any other nation in Europe, and the Crusades had more effect on the national growth of France than on that of any other nation. But in no sense was the first Crusade a national enterprise, and no king took part in it.

At the time of the first Crusade Philip I, the fourth king of the Capetian dynasty, was on the throne of France, and like those of his line who had gone before him he had little power, and no taste for great adventures. William the Red, who had small care for religion, ruled in England. Henry IV, emperor of Germany, was under the ban of the Church, and with the whole Empire in confusion it was not wonderful that neither the emperor nor any great German prince took part in the expedition.

The soldiers from any one country did not march under a national leader. Neither was there any commander-in-chief. There was no discipline, no commissariat, nothing, in fact, which goes to make an army in the modern sense of the word.

Only a wonderful faith and enthusiasm could have set such an army in motion. Only wonderful faith and ignorance could believe in its success. The Crusades did not succeed, and the story of them is the story of one of the most sublime and picturesque failures in all history. But the story of the Crusades themselves hardly belongs to European history. It is the effect upon Europe which matters chiefly, and the fact of success or failure made little difference to this effect, which was very great.

THE CRUSADES: THE CHRISTIAN KINGDOM OF JERUSALEM—THE FOUNDING OF THE GREAT ORDERS OF KNIGHTHOOD

IT was not until the autumn of 1096 that the first great Crusading army set out, and it did not reach Jerusalem until June 1099, nearly three years later. It had indeed been preceded by an unarmed and motley crowd under Peter the Hermit and Walter the Penniless. But these nearly all died of hunger and disease, or by the swords of the enemy, long before they reached Palestine.

Jerusalem yielded quickly to the Crusaders, and a terrible slaughter of the unbelievers took place. The streets ran red with blood, and were piled high with dead. Then, their vengeance satisfied, the Christian knights put off their blood-stained armour, and dressed in white robes, carrying palm branches in their hands, marched to the Church of the Holy Sepulchre to give thanks to God for their great victory.

Kingdom of Jerusalem

A Christian monarchy was then established in Jerusalem, and Godfrey of Bouillon, one of the bravest and wisest of the Crusaders, was chosen king. But he refused to take the regal title, or to wear a crown of gold in the city where the Saviour of the world had worn a crown of thorns. He called himself merely baron and defender of the Holy Sepulchre. Having enthroned their king, and leaving with him a few hundred knights to keep his kingdom from again falling into the hands of the Turks, most of the Crusaders took their way home again.

The new kingdom of Jerusalem was modeled upon the feudal states of western Europe. To set up such a kingdom in the midst of enemies, and so far away from Christian aid that months must elapse before a cry for help could be answered, was a wonderful act of faith. Yet as long as the Crusades lasted the Christian kingdom continued, although at times it was little more than a name. It was perpetually in a state of siege. For although the Crusaders might, from time to time, come in numbers large enough to defeat the Turks, they never remained in numbers large enough to hold the country securely. The Christian kingdom, therefore, depended for its existence chiefly on two powerful orders of knighthood to which the Crusades gave rise, the orders of the Knights of St. John and the Knights Templars.

Knights of St. John or Hospitallers

The Crusades offered many opportunities for the development of chivalry, and of the spirit of devotion. This devotion showed itself in a new way, and brought still another element into war. This new element was chivalry to the wounded. Hitherto men had thought little of the sufferings of those who fell in battle. No knight, at least, would have thought of giving his life to tend the sick. The knight's business was to fight. Yet now there arose an order of knighthood the members of which gave their lives to the nursing of the sick and wounded.

Already some years before the Crusaders took Jerusalem an Italian merchant had founded a hospital there for the benefit of poor and sick pilgrims. It was not indeed a hospital in the modern sense of the word, but rather a guest-house and place of rest for pilgrims. The word comes from the Latin hospitium, the place where in a Roman house the guests were received.

In this hospital many wounded Crusaders found a refuge, and one of Godfrey's first actions after he became king was to visit the hospital. He was so touched by what he saw there that he presented his estates in Brabant to the hospital. Many of his knights following his example gave money and lands to it, and even joined the ranks of its servers. Very soon the abbot of the house proposed that they should form a community, and thus the order of the Knights of St. John was founded.

The members of this order took a threefold vow of celibacy, poverty, and obedience. They were both monks and knights. Their life was henceforth to be spent not in the causing but in the binding up of wounds, and they took as a habit a plain black robe marked with a white cross of eight points.

Before long, however, this peaceful order changed into a military one. For it was hard for men who had been fighters all their lives suddenly to transform into careful nurses. So the knights took a new oath binding themselves to shed the last drop of their blood in the defence of their faith, but never under any circumstances to draw sword in any other cause. They were also now divided into three classes, nobility, clergy, and serving brothers.

Into the first class only he could enter who could show that his family had for two generations at least been noble, and the highest of every land became eager to send their sons to the Hospital of St. John to receive their knightly training. But although the order became a military one, the motive which had originally inspired it was not forgotten. The care of the wounded was still their first duty, and all over the world they became known as the Hospitallers.

The order quickly became wealthy. For every noble who joined its ranks, unable because of his vow of poverty to possess wealth himself, gave all he had to the order. Many others, in gratitude for restored health, bestowed riches upon it, others again, in penance for their sins, bequeathed to it lands and manor houses.

With this wealth the order built hospitals in every part frequented by pilgrims or Crusaders. They bought fleets of ships, and owned whole towns, and at length became so powerful that even kings began to fear them, and be jealous of their wealth and power.

Knights Templars

A little later than the order of St. John another order of monkish knights, the order of the Knights Templars, was founded. They devoted themselves not to the tending of the sick but to protecting unarmed pilgrims on their way to the Holy Land, and were first known as the Poor Soldiers of Christ. But after they were given a house near the Temple of Solomon, they became known as the Knights of the Temple. They took the same monkish vows as the Hospitallers, and wore a white robe marked with a red cross. From this they were also given the name of Red Cross Knights. They were, it was said, "Lions in war, lambs in the house, fierce and unforgiving to the foes of Christ, but kind and gracious to all Christians."

Like the Hospitallers the Knights Templars soon became rich. Soon, indeed, they far surpassed the earlier order in wealth, and forgetting that their first duty was to serve they became the most insolent and proud of all the orders of knighthood, and also the most avaricious. The name of Templar, indeed, almost became a synonym for greed and pride.

Long after the Crusades were over both these orders of knighthood continued to exist. But early in the fourteenth century the Templars were accused of heresy and all manner of evil living, and were crushed out of existence with great cruelty by Philip IV of France. The history of the Hospitallers was much longer than that of the Templars, continuing until disbanded by Napoleon on his way to Egypt in 1798. With that the history of the order really ends, but many attempts were made to reconstitute it. Out of one of these attempts has grown the St. John Ambulance Association, whose special care is for the wounded in war, thus carrying on the first ideals of the parent society, founded more than eight hundred years ago.

The Teutonic Order

In the time of the third Crusade another similar order was founded, and as the members were chiefly German it became known as the Teutonic Order. They took as their habit a white robe with a black cross, and like the order of St. John, this order had its beginnings in a hospital founded by some German merchants. Like the other similar orders, it soon became a great military and trading organization, with fleets and lands, and almost regal power. But the Teutonic Knights played a much greater part in the expansion of Germany than in the conquest of Palestine. Their presence had little influence on the Latin kingdom of Jerusalem, whereas without the support of the Hospitallers and the Templars it could not have continued to exist.

THE CRUSADES
THE LATIN EMPIRE OF CONSTANTINOPLE

THE second Crusade set out about fifty years after the first. Since Urban had preached the first enthusiasm for the Holy War had spread so that even sovereign rulers had become infected by it, and now Louis VII, king of France, and Conrad III, emperor of Germany, became the leaders of the new venture. But this Crusade accomplished nothing.

The Third Crusade

The third Crusade was called forth by the recapture of both Acre and Jerusalem by the Turks. This time three kings led the armies, Richard Cœur de Lion, king of England; Philip II, king of France; and Frederick Red Beard, or Barbarossa, emperor of Germany. Frederick, however, died long before he reached the Holy Land. Philip and Richard went on, and after a siege of nearly two years, they recovered possession of Acre. Then Philip and Richard quarrelled, and Philip went home. Richard lingered on in Palestine, but he could not regain possession of Jerusalem, and at length, after signing a truce of three years with the Sultan, he, too, returned home.

Fourth Crusade

The fourth Crusade had far more effect on Europe than on Palestine. For instead of going to Jerusalem the Crusaders turned aside and took Constantinople.

Isaac II, a weak and degenerate emperor, had been deposed and blinded by his brother Alexius, who caused himself to he crowned as Alexius III. But Isaac's son, a boy of twelve, also named Alexius, escaped from Constantinople, fled to Italy, and there and in other European states begged for help against the usurper. He received it at last from the Crusaders gathered to fight for the city of God.

These Crusaders had already turned from their first purpose, and had helped the Venetians to recover the City of Zara which had revolted from the Republic of Venice, and placed itself under the protection of the king of Hungary. They had done this, too, in spite of the thunders of the pope, who forbade them to touch the city. For the king of Hungary had taken the cross, "and he who attacked a city belonging to him made himself an enemy of the Church," said the pope.

By the time Zara was taken it was too late in the year to go on to Palestine, so the Crusaders passed the winter there. And here came young Alexius to entreat their aid. In return he promised to pay a large sum of money, and in his own and his father's name, swore to put an end to the division between the Greek and the Roman Church, and bring the whole Eastern Empire under the sway of the pope. That, surely, thought the Crusaders, would be a righteous deed, and in spite of some opposition among their ranks, they promised Alexius the help he craved.

The Crusaders attack Constantinople

So in April 1203 the Crusaders set sail. A great company of Venetians joined them also, and Constantinople was attacked both by land and sea, and the great city which had so often withstood the onslaught of heathen and infidel, fell before the host of Christian brigands. Alexius fled, the feeble and now blind emperor Isaac was restored to the throne with his son Alexius IV as co-emperor.

But two such emperors, one blind and decrepit, the other young and utterly frivolous, were ill-fitted to rule the Empire in troublous times. When Alexius tried to fulfil his promise, to bring the Empire under the sway of the pope the people rose in rebellion. During the turmoil the old emperor Isaac died, and Alexius also was slain, his reign having lasted only six months.

A new emperor, Alexius V, was placed upon the throne, but the Crusaders took up arms against him. Constantinople was sacked and burned, and Alexius V fled for his life. Then from among their own number the Crusaders chose another emperor, Baldwin, Count of Flanders.

In the Eastern Empire the feudal system was unknown. The emperors might be despotic or corrupt, but at least their subjects had not to fear the rapine of their fellow-subjects. Now its Latin conquerors endeavoured to introduce the feudal system. The Empire was parcelled out among them, and the emperor became merely a feudal chieftain. The Greek clergy were driven from their churches, and a host of priests and monks were imported from Rome in order to convert the people. For, although the Greeks were Christians, because they did not acknowledge the pope as head of the Church, they seemed to the narrow-minded Crusaders to be infidels, almost as much as the Mohammedans, and in sore need of conversion.

But the task of turning the Eastern Empire into a feudal state, and the Greek Church into an obedient daughter of Rome, proved a task too great for the Latins. There was no sympathy between the rulers and the ruled. The Greeks were worn out and effete, but their learning and culture were far beyond that of their western conquerors. Their ideas of civilization were altogether different. Yet for fifty-seven years the Latin Empire struggled on. Then one day, with a mere handful of soldiers, a Greek general surprised and took Constantinople. The Frankish emperor, Baldwin II, fled away, a Greek emperor (Michael VIII) was once more proclaimed, and the Latin domination of the Eastern Empire came to an end.

Fifth Crusade

The only Crusade after the third which brought any relief to pilgrims to the Holy Land was the fifth. That, strange to say, was followed, not by the pope's blessing but by his curse. For Frederick II, emperor of Germany, who led it, was under the ban of the Church when he set out. That an excommunicated man should dare to fight for the Lord's Tomb seemed a mockery and an insult, a cause not for rejoicing but for sorrow and anger. Yet Frederick succeeded where others had failed. He fought little, but by diplomacy he won a ten years' truce from the sultan, and also the assurance of a safe passage for pilgrims through Palestine to the Holy Places.

Other Crusades followed but they did little for the cause. The passionate enthusiasm which had made the first possible died down. One by one every town which the Crusaders had conquered was again taken from them by the Mohammedans until only Acre was left. At length that, too, fell before the Turks, and in 1291 the Christian kingdom of Jerusalem came to an end.

THE EFFECT OF THE CRUSADES—
THE FALL OF CONSTANTINOPLE

FOR two centuries the Crusades had filled Europe with unrest. The lives of millions of men had been sacrificed, and in the end the Holy Land remained in the possession of the unbeliever. The Crusaders had accomplished nothing of what they had set out to do. But they had wrought great changes in Europe. For one thing they had caused a redistribution of wealth and power. They had helped to weaken the power of the great feudal lords, and they had strengthened that of both kings and peoples.

When the great nobles wanted money to enable them to set out on a Crusade they sold or mortgaged their lands and everything they possessed. To such an extent was this so that King Richard of England declared that he would sell London if he could find a suitable purchaser. In this way many great estates changed hands. Some were bought by churchmen, thus the Church grew stronger. Others came into the hands of the kings, either by purchase, or because the vassal to whom they had been granted never returned from the Holy Land, and they naturally fell to the king as overlord. Thus the kings became stronger.

But most of all the people benefited. In return for money supplied the feudal lords were obliged to grant many privileges to the towns. The burghers began to have new ideas of freedom, manufactures and commerce increased, guilds and corporations were founded, and soon became powerful. For the mere equipment of the great hosts which every now and again took their way towards Palestine necessitated a certain amount of trade and manufacture. The transporting of these same hosts across the seas encouraged shipbuilding. New plants and fruits, such as lemons, apricots, maize, and sugar-cane, were introduced into Europe, through which both agriculture and manufactures were given an impetus.

The villains and slaves, too, profited. For in the absence of the constantly warring nobles they could sow and reap in peace, and life for them became both happier and easier. A few also bought their freedom by following their lord's example and taking the cross. Everywhere thus the bands which had bound society began to loosen, and the great gulf which had separated the upper and the lower classes began to be bridged.

In the nobles themselves changes took place. They had gone forth to fight the infidel, scorning him as a barbarian. Everywhere in the east, both in the Eastern Empire and in the Mohammedan lands, they had found a culture and civilization far greater than their own. Science, especially that of medicine, was far more advanced in the east than in the west. Even in the science of war the Crusaders found that they had something to learn form the despised infidel. In the west it had required a knightly vow to make a man courteous and gentle. Everywhere in the east the Crusaders found a refinement of manners to them undreamed of. They found a love of art and letters, and graces of life, of which before they had had no conception. And although they affected to despise these things they were not without their influence.

Added to this the mere act of travel broadened their minds. Many who joined the Crusades had never before left their own village. They had no consciousness of other lands or peoples. Now, as for weeks they marched through strange countries, their ides of the world became enlarged. They heard of yet other lands far beyond Palestine. The desire to know more of them was awakened and a great impulse was given to the study of geography and of history. Poetic literature, too, received an impulse, and many of the finest mediæval romances have to do with the story of the Crusades.

These changes only came gradually. They were changes which were bound to come, and if the Crusades had never taken place they would have come in time. But the Crusades undoubtedly hastened that time.

The Ottoman Turks

One other office the Crusades performed. That was keeping the Turks out of Europe. For while they were engaged with the Crusades they had no energies to attack the Eastern Empire. And when the Crusades came to an end the Empire of the Seljukian Turks was also tottering to its fall. But its place was soon taken by that of the Ottoman Turks, who had been driven westward by the great Genghis Khan and his successors.

They were at first only a small tribe of pastoral warriors. But they increased rapidly in power, and before the end of the thirteenth century they had become a menace to the Eastern Empire. Bit by bit they wrested from the Greeks what little remained of their possessions in Asia, then they passed into Europe.

On and on they came, farther and farther west. Nothing it seemed could stay their conquering march, and all Christian Europe trembled. Then once more the pope called upon Christian warriors to defend the Church of Christ against the infidel, and the kings of France, Germany, and Hungary, uniting their forces, marched to check the terrible foe. But at the battle of Nicopolis in Bulgaria the Christian army was cut to pieces, and the victorious foe vowed that he would not stay his march until he had stabled his horses in the Church of St. Peter at Rome.

Fall of Constantinople

But before he had time to fulfil his threat the Turk was called back to fight another foe and defend his conquests against the attacks of the terrible Mongol, Tamerlane. The Turks in their turn went down before this fierce conqueror, and the Ottoman power was humbled to the dust. But in a wonderfully short time the Ottomans recovered themselves, and fifty years after their defeat by Tamerlane they, for the last time, laid siege to Constantinople. This time the capital of the Eastern Empire, which had withstood their onslaughts for so many hundred years, fell. The last emperor, named Constantine, like the founder of the Eastern Empire, died fighting for his capital, and the great sultan, Mohammed II, rode in triumph into the Church of St. Sophia.

Thus the Crescent triumphed over the Cross, and an Asiatic and alien people took their place among the nations of Europe. They held sway over a huge territory, including parts of what are now Austria, Hungary, Russia, Greece, Serbia, Rumania, and Bulgaria, besides many other lesser provinces. From the Black Sea to the Adriatic, from the Dniester and the Bug to the Mediterranean, the Crescent flew victorious. Added to this the Ottomans had a great Empire in Asia and Africa, and the Sultan boasted "that he was master of many kingdoms, ruler of three continents, and lord of two seas."

The Ottoman Turks were the last barbarian tribe to settle upon European soil. They did not disappear like the Huns, they were not driven forth like the Saracens, they have in no way become Europeanized like the Hungarians or Magyars, they have remained Asiatic and alien, a blot upon the map of Europe to this day.

THE HOLY ROMAN EMPIRE—
STRIFE WITH THE POPES—
COMMERCIAL PROGRESS

THE Saxon line of emperors came to an end with Henry V (see Chapter XX), and under the Hohenstaufens the bitter struggle between popes and emperors continued. Emperors, too, still strove after world dominion, while their power over Germany was yet unstable.

At length both Germany and Italy became divided into two great parties. In Germany the factions were known as Welfs and Waiblings, in Italy as Guelphs and Ghibellines. The Welfs or Guelphs were followers of the pope, the Waiblings or Ghibellines were followers of the emperor, Waibling being a sort of surname given to the Hohenstaufens from their castle of that name.

Frederick I, Barbarossa

In the tremendous struggle between pope and emperor the Empire was to succumb, but for a time the inevitable end was staved off by the genius of a great man. This was Frederick I, Barbarossa. Strong and just, a great statesman and a great soldier, he was, perhaps, the best emperor who has ever ruled over Germany.

Under him once again the warring states were united. Even he could not entirely put down private warfare but he greatly reduced it, and in the comparative peace the country became more prosperous and united than ever before. It would have been well for Germany had Barbarossa been content with his work there. But once again the desire for world dominion and the fatal connection with Italy brought ruin.

The Normans were by this time firmly established in Italy, and the south was thus practically lost to the Empire. In the north the great cities had grown powerful, and taking advantage of the quarrels between pope and emperor had wrung themselves free and formed republics. The emperors' quarrels with the pope were bitter and frequent, and in these struggles the popes sometimes sought help from the Normans, sometimes from the Lombard cities. They used their spiritual powers against the emperor also, and like some of his predecessors, Barbarossa was excommunicated. But the thunders of the Church did not affect him as they had affected Henry IV. For Barbarossa ruled Germany with a strong hand, and the German bishops were emperor's men rather than pope's men. They did homage to the emperor for their fiefs, and rode with his army. Had the German Church always been thus true to the emperor the fate of the German Empire might have been other than it was.

Italy and the Empire

Soon after his coronation Frederick entered Italy and in several campaigns reduced the Lombard cities to submission. It was done with not a little cruelty, Milan being razed to the ground. He placed German rulers over the cities and provinces and laid upon the people such a burden of taxes that the record of them was called "The book of pain and mourning."

Frederick's first papal quarrel was with Adrien IV, the only Englishman who ever sat upon the papal throne. It began over a very small matter. Adrien wrote a letter to Frederick in which he seemed to claim that the Empire was his (the pope's) gift and the emperor merely his vassal. At this assumption the imperial wrath blazed furiously. The pope was roused to equal fury, and only his death saved the emperor from excommunication.

But his death, far from ending the quarrel, only added more fury to it. For two popes were now elected, the emperor's party choosing Victor IV, the pope's party Alexander III. Each pope, as soon as he was enthroned, excommunicated his rival, and Alexander III also excommunicated the emperor.

Barbarossa cared little for the thunders of the Church. But Alexander was a formidable foe. It was he who later threatened Henry II of England with excommunication for the murder of Thomas à Becket. Against such a pope the emperor needed all his strength, and soon his cause was endangered by the death of his own pope. But nothing daunted, he elected another, Paschal III, and marching on Rome, he took the city, and triumphantly enthroned his pope there, while Alexander fled in dismay.

The emperor had conquered, but in the very moment of his triumph disaster overtook him. Pestilence wasted his army, and the Lombard cities, joining hands with Pope Alexander, rose in revolt. Frederick sent to

Germany for reinforcements, they were refused, and in the battle of Legnano he was defeated by the Lombards.

This battle was a turning point in Frederick's reign. After it he saw that it was useless longer to struggle against the growing spirit of freedom which had grown up among the cities of Italy. So he made peace with the Lombards, keeping only a vague suzerainty over them. He also gave up the cause of the rival pope, and made peace with Alexander, who removed the ban of excommunication from him. Even after this, however, his dealings with the popes were never altogether smooth.

A few years later Frederick made peace with Sicily also, and arranged a marriage between his son Henry and Constance the heiress of Sicily. Thus at length Sicily became a fief of the Empire. The pope, however, was ill-pleased with this last stroke of policy on Frederick's part. For with Sicily a fief of the Empire he lost an ally in his struggles with the emperor. Yet angry although he was he did not renew the ban of the Church.

Three years later Barbarossa set out with the third Crusade, and died somewhere in Asia Minor. But he had impressed himself so thoroughly on the German people that they did not believe in his death. So a legend arose that he was only resting after his great labours, and that he would come again. He sits, it is said, within a cave in the heart of the Kyffhausen Mountains, waiting till his country has need of him.

The emperors who succeeded Barbarossa were all involved in the same old round of struggle—with angry popes, with rebellious German states, with revolting cities in northern Italy—and to all was added the struggle to conquer Sicily securely for the Empire. At length, under the weight of all these evils the Empire was crushed to the dust.

In the days of Otto IV the land was filled with strife. First Otto disputed the crown with Philip of Swabia, and after he was accepted as emperor, Frederick of Hohenstaufen, king of Sicily, appeared as his rival. In this quarrel foreign nations also became involved, King John of England allying himself with Otto, and Philip of France allying himself with Frederick. This was the first international war in the history of Europe. It ended in the triumph of France at the battle of Bouvines (see Chapter XXI).

Otto rode from the field a fallen emperor, and Frederick II took his place. He, at first sustained by the pope, was soon involved in quarrels with him. During his reign four popes ruled in Rome, but his bitterest quarrels were with the two last, Gregory IX and Innocent IV. He was excommunicated more than once, but he was unbending in his defiance, and, to prove his contempt for the pope's authority, while still under the ban of the Church, he insolently undertook the fifth Crusade. Yet this was the only one of the later Crusades which produced the result for which it was initiated.

Frederick was brilliant and learned, a lover of science and art, and his ideas of statesmanship were far before his times. But he was far more a Sicilian than a German, and during his long reign of thirty-five years, although he ruled Sicily well, he neglected Germany and spent little of his time there. Indeed, during the last thirteen years of his reign he never crossed its borders. The German nobles taking advantage of this neglect once more did as they would, and the land was filled with private wars and bloodshed. Yet out of this time of confusion a great trade organization arose in the Hanseatic League.

Hanseatic League

During his reign Barbarossa had greatly encouraged the towns with their trade and commerce, and had made many of them free cities owning allegiance to none but the emperor. Now these towns had no mind to lose their freedom and their trade through the depredations of robber knights. So for protection they banded themselves into leagues, of which the Hanseatic League soon became the chief. It grew to such importance that all the trade of the Baltic, and most of the trade of the North Sea, was soon in its hands. It owned armies and fleets, and even kings were forced to bow to its power.

Much of the trade of England was carried on by the Hanseatic merchants. The English called them Easterlings, or men from the East. They were probably even allowed the privilege of coining English money. From this we have our word sterling, used still in connection with British coinage to express its genuineness and good quality. Thus early the German people, as distinct from the German nobles, showed their aptitude for peaceful commerce. And once again history seems to show that if the emperors had been content to forget their wild dream of world dominion, and advance their country in the ways of peace, the fate of the Empire

114

might have been very different. As it was, because of this dream and the wars with the Popes which were one of its consequences, both the House of Hohenstaufen and the Empire were brought to ruin.

FRANCE: THE CAPTIVITY OF THE POPES—
THE BEGINNING OF THE HUNDRED
YEARS' WAR

UNDER Philip Augustus, France began to take a great place among the nations of Europe (see Chapter XXI). It was another Philip—Philip IV—who broke the power of the pope.

The Hohenstaufen dynasty had been brought to utter ruin through its constant and fierce struggles with the popes. The popes had triumphed. But they had not come forth from the battle altogether unwounded, and in time the papacy declined even as its great rival the Empire declined.

The power of the Hohenstaufens had fallen before the power of the papacy because it had no solid foundation. It was not rooted in nationality. But when the papacy came in contact with the strong and growing nationality of France it fell beneath the yoke.

During the first half of the thirteenth century under Innocent III and his immediate successors the papal power was at its highest. Then the pope acted not merely as the spiritual head of all Christendom but as the overlord of every temporal ruler and as the supreme potentate in Italy. Innocent interfered with the temporal affairs of Europe from Norway to Spain, from England to Hungary. Weak King John of England cowered beneath his wrath, and even Philip Augustus of France, the strongest ruler in Europe at the time, had to bow to his will.

Merely by the force of his tremendous claims, aided by the visionary authority which still surrounded the name of Rome, the pope compelled the submission of mighty kings and princes, without drawing a sword, with indeed no army to back him.

Boniface VIII and Philip IV

But among the growing nationalities of Europe a desire for political independence of the papacy began gradually to make itself felt. When, however, Boniface VIII came to the papal throne he was blind to this fact. He was formed rather to be an emperor than a priest. No pope ever made

116

greater claims to power, and with all the arrogance of his predecessors he plunged into strife with Philip the Fair of France. It began nominally over a question of money.

As the king's power increased, as his activities multiplied, he became always more and more in need of money. But financial science was slow in developing. Indeed, the whole business of government, the best and most equitable means of ruling a people, and binding it together in common interests, had still to be learned. There was no regular system of taxation, and when a king wanted money he raised it how he could, often enough using vile and despotic means.

Now Philip IV, in want of money, laid a tax upon the clergy. This seemed to the pope a usurpation of his rights, and he issued a bull forbidding the clergy to pay any tax to a temporal ruler without his consent. But Philip was not to be thus browbeaten, and he replied by forbidding the export of gold from France, thereby cutting off the pope's revenues from French clergy.

At this the pope, proud although he was, gave way, and for a time peace between the two arrogant rulers was patched up. But the quarrel soon broke out again, this time the pope threatening Philip with excommunication. Philip, however, was no German emperor. He publicly burned the pope's bull, sent him an insulting reply, and called the States General together.

This was a great step towards freedom for the people of France. Ever since the advent of the Capetians parliaments had been held. But they were little more than courts of justice, and to them only the nobles and clergy had been called. Now Philip called to his parliament not only nobles and clergy but the third estate also, that is, burghers, and deputies from the large towns and cities.

Philip was the most absolute monarch who had ruled over France up to this time, and it is possible that in calling the third estate to his parliament he had no thought but of showing his own power. He would show the pope that he could do as he liked within his own kingdom, and that his people were with him.

So he called representatives from the towns to "hear, receive, approve, and do what should be commanded them by the king." He felt that for the moment the support of the people was needed to save him from the fate which had overtaken the German emperors who, without their people's support, had been crushed under the power of the pope. He did not foresee that beneath the power of the people, whose help he now invoked, the French monarchy would one day go down in the dust.

Babylonish Captivity

The support which Philip expected from the people he received. Strong in their strength his defiance of the pope continued, and he even went so far as to make him a prisoner. And when overcome with wrath and shame the aged Boniface VIII died, Philip found means to have a Frenchman set upon the papal throne. This pope of Philip's choosing was Clement V. He was entirely under Philip's influence, and that he should remain so Philip made him take up his residence at Avignon instead of at Rome.

Avignon was a possession of the pope. It was, however, surrounded by French territory, and during the seventy years that Avignon remained the abode of the popes the policy of the Holy See was directed by Frenchmen. This time came to be known as the Babylonish Captivity of the popes, and the fact that such a captivity was possible decreased to an enormous extent the power of the papacy over the nations of Europe.

From this time the glory of the papacy was at an end. It was a shock to the world to find that the great pontiff, who claimed jurisdiction over all princes, could be made the servant of one. A pope living almost in France lost the prestige and the glamour borrowed from the name of Rome. Nation after nation began to realize its capability for independence, and became disinclined to recognize any power beyond the limits of its nationality. The chief European powers, after long struggles, had at last won some unity and solidarity. Factions were disappearing, kings were becoming more powerful, and all classes were growing more obedient to them.

Being able to command obedience from their own subjects, kings and princes cared the less for the mandates of the pope. They obeyed him just as far as they wanted and no farther. Thus with the birth of nationality the power of the pope in secular matters was bound to decrease. In spiritual matters, however, the whole world still acknowledged the pope as supreme.

Throughout his reign Philip not only combated the power of the pope, but also the power of the feudal nobles, and with terrible cruelty he broke up the order of the Knights Templars. But he supported the burgher classes. He was a hard, unlovable man, but his reign was a great one for France.

The Later Capetians

Philip was succeeded by his son Louis X, who after a short reign of eighteen months died, leaving only a daughter to succeed him. Many of the French thought that if this daughter were allowed to reign she would inevitably be sought in marriage by the king of some neighbouring state, and by such a marriage a foreigner would become king of France. The French people were already too much awake to suffer this.

So the States General was called together, and an old law of the Salian Franks which decreed that no woman might inherit land was brought to light. This old law had really nothing to do with the succession to the crown, but it served the purpose. It was decided that because of this law no woman might sit upon the throne of France, and because it was supposed to date from the days of the Salian Franks it was called the Salic Law.

By right of this law then, Philip V succeeded his brother Louis X, and as both he and a third brother, Charles IV, died without male heirs the Capetian dynasty in direct succession died out.

During the three hundred and fifty years that the Capets had ruled they had done much for France. Out of a mass of warring feudal states they had made a compact kingdom. All the great fiefs except Flanders, Brittany, Burgundy, and Guienne had been absorbed by the crown, and with this absorption the power of the feudal nobility was practically put an end to.

The capital, after being moved from place to place, was finally fixed at Paris, and a real, if elementary, system of government was established.

Upon the death of Charles IV, in accordance with the newly adopted Salic Law, the crown devolved upon Philip of Valois, nephew of Philip IV, and cousin of the last three kings. But these three kings, Louis, Philip, and Charles, had a sister Isabella, who had married Edward II, king of England.

Her son, Edward III, now claimed the throne of France, on the ground that even if his mother Isabella could not herself be queen of France, she could transmit the title to a male heir. Therefore, he as grandson of Philip IV, claimed to have a better right to the throne than Philip of Valois, who was merely a nephew.

The Hundred Years' War

Out of this claim there arose what is known as the Hundred Years' War. As a matter of fact, although not altogether continuous, the Hundred Years' War covered a period of a hundred and seventeen years. Its effect, both on England and on France, was so great and enduring that it ranks as one of the great events in the history of the end of the Middle Ages. It continued throughout the reigns of five French and five English kings.

Edward III's claim to the French throne was, however, not the sole cause of the war, it only served as an excuse. So far as the English were concerned the war was not simply a barons' war waged in the interests of regal power. It was for them linked with commerce and the business life of the people.

Flanders was one of the French fiefs which was still outside the French king's influence. Indeed, the Flemish, grown rich by their own industry, had bought large liberties, and many of the towns of Flanders were practically republics. And in trying to amalgamate Flanders with the rest of his kingdom the king of France was forced into war with the haughty and freedom-loving weavers and wool merchants of these communes.

The Flemish resisted the French king's efforts to incorporate them with France because they had no common interests. The interests and fortunes of Flanders and of England were, on the other hand, closely bound together. For it was English wool which kept the Flemish looms busy, and English wool-growers depended for their livelihood almost entirely on the Flemish markets.

The French king's victory over the Flemish merchants would constitute a menace to English trade. For the English, therefore, this war appeared not merely a struggle for kingly power but one with which the interests of the people were bound up. And the memorable victories gained by the English were victories of the people and not of the nobles.

Edward's army was, it may also be noticed, mainly composed not of

120

feudal vassals but of paid soldiers drawn from the lower classes. This was, no doubt, partly from necessity. For a vassal was only bound to serve his lord during a stated number of days. He was often not bound to serve him at all beyond the seas. And as, wearied by his long wars, Edward saw more and more of his nobles turn homeward, he was obliged to fill their places by paid foot soldiers, either volunteers or forced levies.

Added to this, English leaders had already, through their frequent wars with Scotland, begun to learn the value of archers and foot soldiers, and they became actually desirous of having them in their army. But these English-Scottish wars, which had taught the English so much, were of a local character. Little was known of them on the Continent. The French knights knew nothing of the value of archers, and to them Edward's force, deficient as it was in knightly splendour, must have seemed a contemptible little army.

Flemish trade was as much in the balance as English trade. But at first the Flemish communes declared themselves neutral. When, however, the position of armed neutrality became untenable they flung the last vestige of loyalty to the French king to the winds and openly declared their alliance with Edward. This alliance was of great advantage to the English, as it threw the Flemish ports open to them and made the landing of an army much easier that it would otherwise have been.

FRANCE: THE HUNDRED YEARS' WAR

Creçy and the Siege of Calais

THE first important victory of the Hundred Years' War was that of Creçy. There the hungry, ragged English archers and foot soldiers, rough men of the people, laid low the chivalry of France.

Creçy was more than a victory, it was the beginning of a military and social revolution. It showed that the feudal army was hopelessly behind the times, hopelessly inefficient when confronted with science. The superb courage of the French noble was of no avail when confronted with the superior arms and skill of the English peasant. The French at Creçy never got within striking distance of the English, they could not show their prowess with sword or spear, for the arrows of the common soldier laid them low, and their splendid but weighty armour was of no avail against steel-pointed shafts sped with the force of iron muscles.

Hitherto war had been the profession and the pastime of the great. The knight or noble, superbly mounted and clad in glittering steel, had alone counted in battle. To him had been all the honour and glory. The poor man's part had been but to suffer, to see his crops laid low, his cattle slaughtered or driven off, his home laid in ruins. And of his suffering no man took note. He was there to suffer. Creçy was one of the turning-points in the lives of great and humble alike. Henceforth the gospel of the nobility of the sword was no longer received with perfect faith.

From Creçy Edward marched his victorious little army to Calais, to which he straightway laid siege. From the commercial side of the campaign Calais was a most important place: for it was from this port that the French corsairs sailed which did so much damage to English trade.

Archers, however, deadly though they were in a pitched battle, were useless against the enormous stone walls of a medieval fortress. The clumsy engines of assault made to sling stones were hardly of more avail. Gunpowder, indeed, had lately been discovered, and the English dragged two or three cannons about with them; but they were small and quite powerless against the tremendous masonry of the walls.

The only means then of taking the town was by starvation. With dogged determination the English set about it, and after eleven months Calais yielded.

Edward at once turned Calais into an English colony, settling it with several thousand English merchants and their families. It very quickly became of immense importance, both from a military and a commercial point of view. It was henceforth through this town that English armies were poured into France, and being on the borders of Flanders it became also the centre of distribution for the wool trade. For two hundred years it remained an English possession in spite of strenuous efforts on the part of the French to recover it. When at length it was regained, the loss made little difference to England. It was only of value to them during the aggressive and wholly unjustifiable wars of the Middle Ages.

For some years the pope, Clement VI, had been trying to mediate between the kings of France and England. But he had joined with his efforts an endeavour to extend his power over the English Church, and Edward had received his advances coldly. Now, however, pleased with the result of his campaign, he listened to Clement, and a nine months' truce was signed. But no lasting peace could come of it. For Edward, flushed with victory, was not in a mood to resign any of his claims; he still called himself king of France and denied Philip's right to the title.

But the truce was destined to last longer and men were to have little heart for war. In 1348 a pest, more baneful even than the sword, swept over Europe from the East. This dreadful pestilence, known as the Black Death, wiped out in France and England nearly a half of the population.

Battle of Poitiers

In 1350 Philip VI died and was succeeded by his son John. Under him the war continued, and ten years after Crecy the battle of Poitiers was fought. Except that the pride of chivalry suffered an even greater defeat it was but a repetition of Crecy. At Poitiers King John of France had one of the most magnificent of feudal armies about him. All he had to do was to surround the little English army brought against him, and starve it into surrender.

But that was not the chivalrous manner of waging war. The nobles were anxious to wipe out the shame of Crecy in brilliant fashion. Merely to starve an army into surrender could bring no renown. So once again the chivalry of France pitted itself against the English peasantry. Once again the uselessness of unscientific courage was proved, and the knight went down before the churl.

The flower of French nobility lay dead upon the field. The king himself was taken prisoner to England, there "to enjoy the insolent courtesy" of his captors. But in spite of Crecy, in spite of Poitiers, the conquest of France was as far off as ever. Every feudal castle was a fortress, and the development of the art of fortification had far outdistanced the invention of siege machines. Almost the only means of reducing a fortress was by starvation or by treachery. An army might sit down for months before a fortress, and when at last the endurance of the defenders was exhausted and they yielded, the conquerors only found themselves master of a few more miles of territory, and the business of reducing the next fortress had to be begun.

Even had it been possible by siege after siege to win the country it would have been impossible to hold it. After a time then, weary of sieges, the English left the cities alone and ravished the land, making it a desert. For four years they marched up and down practically unhindered, burning, plundering, and destroying, until the once rich country was a wilderness of ashes and blood-stained ruins.

The Black Death had already carried off hundreds and thousands, and added to this the land was torn by civil wars, the nobles fighting among themselves, and the peasants, driven mad by misery, rising against the nobles.

Treaty of Bretigny

The unhappy people, pushed at length to desperation, yielded to Edward's demands, and by the Treaty of Bretigny half of France south of the Loire was given up to the English. It was given, too, not as a fief but to be held outright "in the manner in which the kings of France had held it." On his side Edward resigned his claim to the throne of France, and for a time there was peace.

It was, however, only exhaustion which had made France yield to the English yoke. Nine years later, when the country had to some extent recovered from that exhaustion, Charles V, who had succeeded his father in 1364, found an excuse for rejecting the Treaty of Bretigny, and the Hundred Years' War broke out again. It now entered upon a new phase.

Edward III had to a great extent lost his Flemish allies, he was old, and his great general and son, the Black Prince, was ill. On the French side Charles V, the politic and not over-chivalrous king, was aided by the military genius of Du Guesclin. So, for a time, all went well with France, and misfortune after misfortune pursued the English, until at length little of Edward's conquests remained save Bordeaux, Bayonne, and Calais.

But Charles V died at the age of forty-six, leaving his son, a child of twelve, to succeed him, and France fell once more on evil days. During the minority of Charles VI the country was torn by strife between the nobles, who quarrelled for the power of regent. Then he, scarce grown to manhood, became insane, and once more the country drifted fast into civil war.

Renewal of the War by Henry V

It was then that Henry V, the young and ambitious king of England, determined to reassert the English claim to the crown of France. Once again at Agincourt the story of Creçy and of Poitiers was repeated, and fifteen thousand English archers defeated an army of fifty thousand knights and nobles. After this prodigious victory Henry's army was, however, too exhausted to do more, and he led it back to England.

In spite of the English menace civil war continued in France. When Henry returned with a fresh army he was encouraged by the rebels, and in 1420 the poor, mad king was forced to sign the Treaty of Troyes. By this Treaty Charles VI gave his daughter Catharine in marriage to Henry, and acknowledged him as his heir, thus disinheriting his own son Charles, and making a gift of the French crown to a foreigner.

Henry, however, never became king of France, for he died in 1422 a little less than two months before his father-in-law. And although upon the death of Charles VI the baby king of England, Henry VI, was proclaimed in Paris as in England, many of the French rejected him. The Dauphin also was proclaimed as Charles VII, and the miserable war dragged on.

GERMANY
CONTINUED STRUGGLES WITH THE POPE

WITH the death of Frederick II (see Chapter XXVII) the Mediæval Empire may be said to end. After him came Conrad IV, the last of the Hohenstaufens, and the Great Interregnum, when for a space of nineteen years there was no real emperor, and the crown was bandied about among foreign princes. Then followed a period of a hundred and sixty-four years, when the crown passed from one house of nobles to another, in all ten emperors. During this time the borders of the Empire shrank considerably. Italy was entirely lost. In the north the great trading cities became independent republics, the middle was held by the pope. In the south the kingdoms of Sicily and Naples were conquered by Charles of Anjou. He was called in by Pope Urban IV to crush the Hohenstaufens, and by him Conradin, the last of the German-Norman kings, was put to death.

Poland became an independent monarchy and rendered no more allegiance to the German crown. Denmark and Hungary also became free of the Empire. To the emperors there remained only Germany itself. It was a Germany more hopelessly divided than ever. While every other kingdom in Europe had been moving steadily towards united nationality, Germany had moved in the opposite direction and now contained two hundred and seventy-six independent states.

The rulers of these states were constantly at variance with each other. They were always ready to fight each other, but never to combine and fight a foreign foe. There was no sense of nationality among them, and their loyalty to their overlord the emperor was of the slightest. These overlords still regarded themselves as emperors, but for two centuries few went to Rome to receive the crown at the hands of the pope, and after the middle of the fifteenth century none did so. As kings they had little power, they had no capital, and no government worthy of the name. Thus striving for world dominion the emperors ceased even to rule in Germany.

During this time the power of the electors who chose the emperor grew rapidly. In early days the emperors had been elected by the whole of the nobles. But by degree most of them lost this right, which was at last usurped by seven men only, three churchmen and four nobles. The churchmen were the archbishops of Mainz, Cologne, and Treves. The nobles were the King of Bohemia, the Margrave of Brandenburg, the Duke of Saxony, and the Count Palatine. In the seventeenth century the princes of Bavaria and of Hanover were added, making the number of electors nine.

As time went on the power of these electors increased enormously, until at length they claimed to be the seven pillars upon which the Empire rested. They forced the emperor of their choice to agree to any conditions they liked to impose. If he tried to go his own way they waged war against him, and sometimes even deposed him. And in this they always found a friend in the pope, to whose advantage it was to have a weak emperor on the throne.

Lewis IV

In 1313 the electors could not agree and two emperors were elected, Lewis IV and Frederick the Handsome. In consequence the land was torn with civil war for many years. The popes were by this time living in Avignon, little more than vassals of the French king. Yet Pope John XXII still tried to impose his will upon Germany. He more or less took the part of Frederick and commanded Lewis to give up the crown in three months under pain of excommunication.

Lewis replied with fury. The election of a German king he declared lay with the German people only and needed no sanction from the pope. As to the quarrel between the two rival emperors, that should be settled by the sword and not by the pope's decree. It was so settled, and after long years of warfare Lewis became reconciled to Frederick and agreed to share the throne with him.

Lewis then marched to Rome, deposed John, and enthroned an anti-pope of his own choosing. At first the Roman people received him with joy. But soon their mood changed, and anti-pope and emperor alike fled for their lives. In 1330 Frederick died, and three years later Lewis, weary of the long conflict, tried to make peace with the pope. He declared himself willing to be recrowned by the rightful pope, and do any penance that he should lay upon him.

But Benedict XII, who had now succeeded John XXII, asked too much. He demanded that Lewis should give up the imperial title until the

127

Church should decide whether he had a right to it or not. At this both the emperor and the electors were filled with wrath, and they issued a solemn manifesto in which they declared that the emperor took his rank and crown from them, and that there was no need whatever for confirmation from the pope. Thus the independence of the Empire from all papal interference was made legal.

Charles IV

But although the princes of Germany had by this manifesto at last shown some dawning loyalty the popes clung obstinately to their powers, and in 1346 Clement VI deposed Lewis and called upon the electors to choose another emperor. By this time the electors were weary of Lewis, and they obeyed the pope and chose Charles the son of the blind king of Bohemia.

This happened in July. In August the battle of Creçy was fought, and in it both King John and his son Charles fought on the side of France. King John was killed, and Charles fled back to Germany. Here once again the land was torn with civil strife. For Charles was not the choice of the people. They felt that he had been imposed by the pope, and called him "a priest's king," and would have nothing to say to him.

Then in 1347 Lewis died, and the crown went begging. It was offered to Edward III of England, refused by him and one German prince after another, and finally by dint of enormous bribes secured by Charles.

During his reign Germany, like the rest of Europe, was devastated by the Black Death, which carried off nearly half the inhabitants. It was followed by a terrible persecution of the Jews who, according to the superstition of the times, were believed to have caused the plague. But "Germany," said a later emperor, Maximilian I, "never suffered from a more pestilent plague than the reign of Charles IV." He utterly neglected Germany, but did everything in his power to aggrandize his own kingdom of Bohemia.

On the other hand he issued a great document, which from the colour of its seal has come to be known as the Golden Bull of Charles IV. It was a document almost as important for Germany as the Magna Carta for England, forming as it did the groundwork of the laws for more than four hundred years.

One of its chief aims was to put an end to strife over the election of the emperor. By it the electors were made still more important. They were given full sovereign rights in their own lands. They could coin money, levy taxes, and make war as they chose. From their courts of justice there was no appeal even to the emperor, and the smallest crime against their persons was punishable as high treason. They were thus raised far above all other princes of the realm. Taken together they were far more powerful than the emperor himself. In the whole Bull there was no mention of the pope and his claims, or even of Italy.

FRANCE: THE END OF THE HUNDRED YEARS'
WAR—THE REIGN OF LOUIS XI

AT the beginning of the fifteenth century France was in a pitiable state. The horrors of the Civil War (see Chapter XXIX), the crimes it had induced, seemed to have crushed out all national spirit. So much so was this that the noxious Treaty of Troyes aroused little opposition. Few realized the national humiliation it involved, and at first it was received almost everywhere with something like satisfaction. Yet from the degradation of the Treaty of Troyes and its consequences France was to awake to true nationality.

In 1422 two kings held sway over France. In Paris, John Duke of Bedford ruled in the name of his baby nephew, Henry VI of England. At Bourges Charles VII of France established himself. The latter seemed far the weaker of the two. Only a small portion of France in the valley of the Loire was true to him, his army consisted chiefly of foreign hired troops, and the English contemptuously called him king of Bourges. They feared him not at all, but they determined to wrest from him all that he had, and they laid siege to Orleans.

Charles was vacillating and weak, and while Orleans struggled in the toils of the foe he idled uncertainly at the castle of Chinon. But now at length France found its soul as a nation. Patriotism awoke. A few years before one part of France had not greatly cared if another part had been devasted. One town had not greatly cared if another was besieged. Now Orleans was besieged, and all France cared, under the yoke of the foreigner although it was. The people of France cared, and in their cottages the peasants wept for the sorrows of their king and country, and armed only with their scythes and axes, they rose against the hated foreigner.

Joan of Arc

In the village of Domremy on the borders of Burgundy and Lorraine, there lived a simple peasant girl named Joan of Arc. All her short life she had heard of war and disaster, of divisions among the nobles, of invasion by a foreign foe. Now she heard how the rightful king of France was an outcast in his kingdom, denied his just inheritance by that foe.

She thought and dreamed of all these things, until at length she seemed to hear the voices of the saints calling her to go forth to save her country and her king. At first she feared to listen to these voices. Then, greatly daring, she determined to obey what seemed to her a heaven-sent command.

So she set forth on the long and perilous journey across the war-ridden land. God protected her and she reached the castle of Chinon in safety. She found it hard at first to make the king believe in her mission; but she was so filled with holy enthusiasm and devotion that none who came in contact with her could long remain unbelieving. Joan of Arc therefore was accepted as a soldier and a leader, and set forth for Orleans.

All that the awakened patriotism of France required was a leader who could command unquestioning obedience and direct its disunited efforts. Only a miracle was needed, and the miracle happened. Under the leadership of a girl of eighteen the undisciplined herd of nobles and their followers became a fighting machine. Men brutalized by long warfare became gentle as doves and fierce as lions. They swore no more, but they fought as if inspired. Before long Orleans was relieved, Charles VII was crowned at Reims, and the Maid's work was done. But she was not allowed to go back, to her peaceful village life as she desired, and in May of 1430 she fell into the hands of the enemy. By them she was cruelly burned as a witch.

This brutal act availed them nothing. The English and their Burgundian allies might kill the Maid, they could not kill her glorious work. For little more than a year only she had led France, but she had led it successfully to nationality and victory. The English cause was dead from the moment Joan of Arc carried her white banner into Orleans. So, in spite of weakness, divisions, intrigues, and even civil war, the English were, by slow degrees, driven out of France. At length only Calais remained to them, and the Hundred Years' War was at an end.

Earlier in this same year, Constantinople had fallen before the Turks, and they had laid hold of a great part of eastern Europe. That they were able to do so was due greatly to the enfeebled state of the Holy Roman Empire, and in part to the exhausted state of France. The emperor did little to stay the triumphant march of the Turks. France, which all through the Crusades had taken a leading part in combating their power, was too stricken and exhausted now, to attempt a crusade against their aggression.

This was a misfortune for eastern Europe, but it was well for France. Instead of frittering away strength upon foreign warfare, she turned to the work of national reconstruction and of regaining her high place among the powers of Europe.

France had suffered much during the Hundred Years' War, but it had gained much. It gained more than it lost, for out of the necessity of combining against a common foe a nation was born, and the nation redeemed itself. But its redemption was not due to monarchical power. It was due to the people who, during the long struggle, had begun to assert themselves. Without their awakened patriotism Charles, vacillating and mediocre as he was, could have accomplished nothing. He has been given the surname of the Victorious, but also that of the Well Served. The latter is, perhaps, the better name. He was well served by his people.

But the great strength of the French monarchy was only latent, and when peace was restored that strength awoke. Under the weight of it the dawning liberties of the people were blotted out, and from this time onward the kingly power in France increased until at length it became an intolerable tyranny against which, at the bitter end, the people revolted.

Louis XI

Under Charles VII France wrung itself free from a foreign yoke. Under his son, that sinister genius, Louis XI, it became a great monarchy. Louis XI may be called the first king of modern France. The kings who had gone before him had been mediæval. Louis was modern. There was no mediaeval glamour about his court, and although he ruled like a tyrant, it was with the cool-headed tyranny of a lawyer, and not with the brutal arrogance of a feudal lord.

Louis was brave, but he never fought an enemy openly if he could gain his end in any other way. That many of his ways were tortuous mattered little to him. "He who does not know how to deceive does not know how to reign," was the sole maxim which he was at the pains to teach to his son the Dauphin.

To him war was a clumsy weapon, to be used only in the last resort. Money, and the power of a fair, if false, tongue, he esteemed much more. He was always ready to pledge his word, and unscrupulous in breaking it if he could gain thereby. He thought that every one had his price, and was willing enough to pay the price in order to win him to his side.

Government was a science to Louis, and he determined that there should be no power in France save the king's power. So he crushed the feudal nobles, both great and small, out of existence, and took possession of their lands. He taught them, by severe measures, that no man had the right to disturb the peace of the realm, or make alliance with the king's enemies.

He laid upon the people a burden of taxes hardly to be borne, but he granted to the burgher classes many privileges. This he did through no love of them, but merely that he might make use of them. To him men were but pawns in his great game, and he did what he would with them. Wily, perfidious, and cruel, he went his way alone, the States General being called together only once throughout his reign.

He was feared by all, loved by few, but he left France united, and with her borders defined and secured as they had never been before. With him the Middle Ages may be said to end.

THE MOORS DRIVEN OUT OF SPAIN—
SPAIN BEGINS TO COUNT AMONG
THE NATIONS OF EUROPE

EARLY in the eighth century the Arabs overran Spain and took almost complete possession of it (see Chapter VII). But although Arabia was the birthplace of Mohammed, the Arabians were less fanatical than any other of the followers of the Prophet. They did not insist on a wholesale conversion of the conquered people. For they loved the Christian's gold more than his conversion. So on condition of paying a tax Christians were allowed to follow their own religion. Nearly all the nobles accepted this condition, but many of the people also became Mohammedan, especially the slaves. For by professing Mohammedanism a slave earned freedom.

But although nearly all Spain came under the domination of the Arabs, a small portion did not. In the extreme north-west, among the Asturian mountains, a few of the inhabitants held out against the invaders. Mountains have always been the last resort of a conquered people, and the Mohammedans were never able to dislodge this remnant from their strongholds. As years passed, indeed, these Spaniards, as we may now call them, strengthened their hold upon the north. Bit by bit they drove the Saracens southward, and at length several little kingdoms were formed, such as Navarre, Leon, Aragon, and Castile, the last taking its name from the many castles built to defend it against the Saracens.

These kingdoms were all small, and all disunited, but by degrees, through marriages between the various royal families and in other ways, several became united in the twelfth century into the kingdom of Aragon, and in the thirteenth century eight little states were united into the kingdom of Leon and Castile.

In the twelfth century also, under Alfonso I, Portugal became a kingdom with a territory less than half its present size. But both Alfonso and his successors fought persistently against the Saracens, and in 1250 Alfonso III conquered what is now the southern portion of Portugal from them, so that from the middle of the thirteenth century the boundaries of Portugal have been very much what they are to-day.

After the union of the various small Spanish states into kingdoms the conquest of Spain from the Moors went on rapidly, and by 1265 all that was left to them was Granada in the extreme south. And even that was not a free kingdom, for the king of Granada owned the king of Castile as overlord.

For more than two hundred years from this time the king of Aragon and the king of Castile ruled over Spain side by side. But as yet there was little sense of Spanish nationality. The two kings were rivals and often enemies. Their kingdoms were merely a conglomeration of small states, the inhabitants of which spoke different languages and had little in common with each other. There were among them Moriscoes or converted Saracens, Marranes or converted Jews, and Mozarabes, Spaniards who had become Mohammedans. To reconcile all these and make them into one nation was no easy matter, yet slowly Spain moved towards nationality.

Ferdinand and Isabella

At length in 1469 Isabella of Castile married her cousin Ferdinand of Aragon, and thus the two crowns were united. But the union of the crowns alone did not satisfy Ferdinand and Isabella. They desired true national union, and they became persuaded that the only way to ensure this was to unite all their peoples into one national Church. In order to do this the Inquisition was introduced into Spain.

The Inquisition was a tribunal of the Church called into being to find out and punish all heretics. It grew up gradually, and was not instituted with all its cruel methods until the thirteenth century. It was a terrible institution, and one from which there was neither appeal nor escape. Every one accused before the tribunal was presupposed guilty, and those who would not at once confess their guilt were tortured until they did. Fines and imprisonment, the forced undertaking of pilgrimages, or the wearing of opprobrious garments were the lightest punishments to which the guilty were condemned, while hundreds and thousands were burned to death with horrible cruelty.

Until the Inquisition was introduced, Spain, with its strangely mixed population, had been more tolerant in the matter of religion than any country in Europe. In their day of power the Moors and Saracens had been tolerant. When their day of power came, the Christians also were tolerant and allowed both Jews and Mohammedans to follow their own religion in peace.

Zealous religious fervour was not at this time a characteristic of Spain. The Spaniards took no part in the Crusades, and none of the rulers of the many little Spanish states appeared before the walls of Jerusalem. This was partly due to the fact that during the period of the Crusades the Spaniards were busy fighting the Saracens at their own doors, reconquering Spain from them.

But these wars between Spaniards and Saracens were national rather than religious. The Spaniards desired to free Spain from the usurper rather than to convert the infidel. So when the Saracens were conquered they were left more or less in peace to follow their own religion. The rulers, indeed, openly recognized the religious rights of their Mohammedan subjects, and one of the kings of Castile took the title of Emperor of all the Spains and of the Men of the Two Religions. But the popes had long looked upon this tolerance as wicked laxness, and at length Isabella, who was deeply and earnestly religious, was persuaded to allow the Inquisition to be set up in Castile.

In everything else Isabella was a great and wise ruler. But in the eyes of later generations this one act has dimmed the splendour of her reign. She must, however, be judged not as a ruler of to-day but as a ruler of the fifteenth century. All Europe was full of religious fanaticism. To the noblest and purest of Churchmen persecution seemed a glorious work for Christ. How then should a mere woman set her tender heart in opposition to their wisdom. So for the glory of God, and for the exaltation of the Catholic Faith, Isabella signed the deed by which the fires of persecution were lit in Spain—fires which were not to be extinguished for hundreds of years. Even in the beginning of the eighteenth century the "question by torture" was still in use, and only in 1834 was the Inquisition finally and utterly abolished.

Besides uniting all Spain into one Church, Ferdinand and Isabella determined to wrest the last inch of the soil from the Mohammedans, and they declared war against the king of Granada. The queen threw herself heart and soul into this war. She appeared in the field fully dressed in armour, encouraging the troops with brave words and reviewing them frequently. She visited every part of the camp, and saw that the soldiers were provided not only with necessaries but with comforts. Above all, she cared for the sick and the wounded.

By her orders large tents known as the Queen's tents were set up in the camps. These were furnished with nurses and medicines, at her expense, and there the sick and wounded could find rest and care. This is believed to be the first attempt at a camp hospital.

Fall of Granada

For ten years the war with the Moors dragged on, the Spaniards often meeting with reverses. But at length civil war broke out in Granada itself. Weakened by strife within as well as war without, the Moors could no longer stand their ground, and on November 25, 1491, Granada yielded. The last Moorish king gave up the keys of the Alhambra Palace to the conquerors. Then, mounting his horse, he rode away. Upon a hill above the city of Granada he drew rein, and with tears in his eyes turned to look for the last time upon his lost capital.

"Yea," cried his mother scornfully, as she watched him, "weep like a woman for the loss of thy kingdom, since thou couldst not defend it like a man." Crushed by his foes, despised by his friends, the Moor bowed his head, and rode forth into exile.

The long struggle between Moors and Spaniards which had lasted for nearly eight hundred years was thus ended. Spain from the Pyrenees to the Mediterranean was now under Christian rule, and for their zeal in the cause of the faith the pope bestowed upon Ferdinand and Isabella the title of the Catholic Kings. This title is to-day still borne by the king of Spain.

Up to this time, because of the continual warfare with the Moors, Spain had entered but little into the life of Europe. It had been untouched by the great movements which had helped to develop the other great states of western Europe. The feudal system had never gained a footing there; as a nation it had never taken part in the Crusades, and had remained unmoved by the tremendous religious enthusiasm which had swept over other countries.

Now late in the day that enthusiasm awoke in the Spanish rulers, and was turned to religious fanaticism and intolerance. With the passing of years this fanaticism increased until, from being the most liberal, Spain became the most intolerant of Catholic states. Persecution began with the Jews.They were offered the hard choice of denying their faith or of leaving the country, and many chose the latter course. Next came the turn of the remaining Moors, they being offered the same hard choice; most of them, like the Jews, chose to go into exile rather than deny their faith. The departure of both these peoples was a loss to Spain. For they were clever and industrious, and much of the trade and any manufactures there were lay in their hands.

This was all the greater loss as now Spain began to be of importance in Europe. The royal family was allied by marriage with other ruling houses of Europe, and Ferdinand is said to have been the first monarch to send resident ambassadors to the courts of other states. By this means friendly intercourse with neighbouring countries was established and maintained, international trade was encouraged, and as the custom increased, quarrels which before could only have been wiped out in blood were settled by negotiation. And however much the maintaining of ambassadors at foreign courts has been abused in later times, in the beginning it was a step towards international understanding and towards lessening the frequency of wars.

CHANGES IN EUROPE CAUSED BY THE DISCOVERY OF THE NEW WORLD

IN the fifteenth century Spain and Portugal were, so to speak, new countries. They had only newly been admitted into the family of Europe. Their own constant wars with the Moors had left them no time to join in the wars and politics of Europe. Their religious toleration had kept them free from papal influences. They had not even joined to any great extent in the commerce of Europe. For of all the countries of western Europe they were in the least advantageous position for trade. They were, as it were, at the end of the world.

All trade was with the East. The Mediterranean was the great trade route. Ports near the centre of this route with good water-ways and roads behind them, by which goods could be distributed throughout Europe, were likely to prosper. Thus Genoa and Venice grew into wealthy and powerful merchant republics. Spain, at the extreme west end of the route, with water-ways short and of little use commercially, cut off, moreover, from the rest of the continent by the Pyrenees, in spite of a Mediterranean seaboard, shared little in its commerce. Aragon, indeed, to some extent, did take part in the commerce of the world, and the ships of Barcelona carried many a rich cargo. But Castile, even after the union of the crowns of Castile and Aragon, did not benefit by this at all. For although it had some Mediterranean seaboard it had no good port. Portugal, having no Mediterranean seaboard, and the ports of the North Sea and the Baltic being for the most part in the hands of the Hansa merchants, was almost entirely cut off from the trade of the world.

But in the fifteenth century, vigorous in their new-found nationality, both Portuguese and Spaniards began to seek outlets for their energies. Such outlets were not easy to find. For Venice controlled the ports of Syria and of Egypt, and the route to India by way of the Red Sea. Since the fall of Constantinople Christian traders had been driven from the Black Sea and the trade routes to Asia in that direction. Indeed, as years went on, the Turks hampered more and more all expansion of Christian trade eastward.

Henry the Navigator

The Portuguese, therefore, were obliged to seek an outlet in another direction. The idea occurred to some of the more daring spirits that it might be possible to reach India by sailing round Africa. So they began, timidly at first, and then more boldly, to explore the west coast of Africa. The way to India was not discovered, but a lucrative trade in negroes and gold-dust rapidly grew up. Year by year in their gay little boats the Portuguese ventured farther and farther afield. The Canary Islands, Madeira, and the Azores were all discovered, or rather rediscovered, for they had been known to the ancients. Soon they were to some extent colonized, and their products, such as honey, maize, and fruits, were added to the growing trade of Portugal.

In all these discoveries and adventures in colonization the Portuguese were encouraged and helped by Prince Henry of Portugal who, because of his enthusiasm in these matters, has been given the name of Henry the Navigator. His great ambition was to find the way to India by rounding Africa. But headland after headland along the coast was passed, and still there seemed no end to it, and Henry died with his dream unfulfilled.

At length the new way to India was discovered by accident. Driven by a storm Bartholomew Diaz rounded the Cape of Good Hope, and sailed some way up the eastern coast of Africa. As it was a storm which had led to his discovery Diaz called the Cape the Cape of Storms. But when he returned home with his news, and men became assured that at last the new way was found to India and the lands of spice, they changed the name to the Cape of Good Hope.

Ten years, however, passed before the attempt to reach India by that route succeeded. Then Vasco da Gama rounded the Cape, steered across the Indian Ocean, reached India, and returned to Lisbon in triumph with a rich cargo. But before this a still more wonderful voyage had been made. Christopher Columbus had sailed across the Atlantic, discovering, as he thought, yet another way to India.

Christopher Columbus

The ancients had believed that the world was flat. But gradually many people had come to think that it was round. Among these was Christopher Columbus, the Genoese sailor. This being so, it must be possible, he argued, to reach India by sailing west just as easily as by sailing east. If this way could be found all the dangers from Mohammedan pirates, all the difficulties of land transport across the desert, from the Red Sea to the Mediterranean, would be avoided, and great fame and fortune would accrue to the people who should find and make use of the new way.

Columbus was filled with a passionate belief in his theory. But he was only a poor man, and had neither the power nor the money needed to fit out an expedition of discovery. So he spent long years in a fruitless endeavour to enlist the sympathy of those who were wealthy and powerful. He carried his great idea first to the court of Portugal and then to that of Spain. But everywhere he was met with prejudice and disbelief. Kings and courtiers alike looked upon him as a crazy adventurer. At length, however, he gained the ear of Queen Isabella. She became fired with something of his own enthusiasm, and promised him the aid he needed.

So at last, on August 3, 1492, Columbus set out on his perilous adventure. To most people, indeed, the adventure seemed not only perilous but mad, and they never expected to see any of those who took part in it again. But in little more than seven months Columbus returned triumphant, having proved the truth of his theory, and found, as he thought, a new way to India. He had done something much more wonderful. He had discovered a new world. But although Columbus made several voyages across the Atlantic, and even landed on the continent of South America, he never discovered his mistake. He died believing that his great title to fame was in having discovered a new way to India.

New Trade Routes

The exploration of the west coast of Africa, the discovery of the route to India by way of the Cape of Good Hope, and the discovery of the lands beyond the Atlantic, completely changed the face of Europe. The ocean and not the Mediterranean became the chief trade route, and the merchant cities such as Venice and Genoa lost their importance. The countries fronting the Atlantic were no longer at the end of the world, but in its centre. Spain, Portugal, the Netherlands, and England became the great sea-going and, therefore, the great commercial nations of Europe.

Spain and Portugal, indeed, tried to shut out all other lands from a share in the new commerce. Soon after Columbus returned from his first voyage the Spanish persuaded Pope Alexander VI to issue a bull which gave to them all heathen lands which had been, or might be, discovered west of an imaginary line drawn from pole to pole, west of the Azores and

Cape Verde Islands. All lands discovered east of this line were to belong to Portugal. But powerful although the pope was, other lands were not easily persuaded to allow Spain and Portugal to reap all the rich harvest of the seas. In 1496 Henry VII of England sent Cabot across the Atlantic to claim for England any lands he might find. The French, too, disregarded the pope's bull. "I fain would see Father Adam's will," cried King Francis of France, "wherein he made you the sole heirs of so vast an inheritance," and he, too, sent out explorers to claim lands for France.

But in the new prosperity which resulted in this sea-going activity the Netherlands for a time took the lead. For Spain and Portugal were busy strengthening their hold on the Indies, England had its domestic troubles, and France was wasting its energies on a dream of dominion in Italy. So most of the carrying trade fell to the share of the Netherlands, and Antwerp for a time took the place which Venice had once held as the centre of the world's commerce.

Soon among the sea-going nations there grew up a keen rivalry for possession of the new lands which every day were being discovered, and wars arose out of this rivalry. Nations fought in Europe for supremacy in the New World. Politics and commerce became strangely mixed, and it is hard to know sometimes where the ambition of kings ends and the enterprise of commerce begins.

THE PROGRESS OF RUSSIA

IN all the new activity and expansion which was taking place in Europe at this time three powers took no part. These were Russia, Italy, and Germany. Italy and Germany, by reason of their wars and discord, Russia because it had not yet risen above the horizon.

After the foundation of Russia by the Northmen (see Chapter XIII) it had, in the thirteenth century, been conquered by the fierce Tartar hordes who swept into Europe from Asia. For more than two hundred years these Tartars held Russia in subjection, and the proud princes, who traced their descent from Rurick the Northman freebooter, were forced to pay tribute to their Asiatic conquerors. But at length the Tartar rule began to weaken, a spirit of resistance awoke among the Russians, and after a fierce and long struggle they threw off the yoke of Asia.

The princes of Moscow were the first to break the domination of the Tartars. Moscow, in consequence, became the capital, and the whole of Russia took the name of Muskovy. Then, having broken the power of the Tartars, the princes of Moscow set themselves to unite Russia under one sceptre. This was done by Ivan III the Great, his son Basil III, and his grandson Ivan IV the Terrible, their three reigns stretching over a period of a hundred and twenty-two years (1462-1584).

So much of this work of union was done by Ivan the Great that he received the name of Binder of the Russian Lands. But in order to bind the land together he crushed out lesser rulers with an utterly ruthless hand, and indeed deserved the name of Terrible almost as much as his grandson.

Basil III followed in his father's footsteps, although he was neither so brilliant nor so ruthless. He consolidated his dominions, and added to them. All he did he did as an autocrat, throwing into prison, and cutting off the heads of any who dared to question his will or authority. And when he died, leaving a child of three to succeed him, the land was once more given over to anarchy and confusion.

Ivan IV, the Terrible

While the great nobles fought for power the future terrible czar wandered about neglected and forsaken. He was clothed like a beggar, and often knew what it was to be hungry as well as cold and lonely. But utterly neglected though he was he learned to read, and his favourite books were the Bible and books of history. In all the books he read the Jewish kings, the rulers of Babylon and Egypt, the emperors of Rome and. Greece, were called czars, and little Ivan determined that he also should be called czar. So he read, and thought, and bided his time. Then when he was seventeen he ordered preparation for his coronation to be made, and insisted on being crowned not as Grand Duke but as Czar of all the Russias.

It was already a large territory over which this first of all the czars now began to rule. But it had one great defect. It was almost entirely an inland country. Save for the Arctic Ocean, it had no seaboard at all. All the shores of the Baltic were in the hands of Swedes, Poles, and of the Brothers of the Sword, a German military order founded to convert the heathen of the Baltic, but which, at the same time, carried on constant wars of aggression against Russia, and played a great part in the expansion of Germany eastwards. In the south, Russia was shut out from the Black Sea and the Caspian by the Mongols. Here we see the reason why Russia took no part in the great seafaring adventures which were stirring western Europe. Hemmed in from the sea on every side by jealous neighbours, and at the same time struggling towards unity, the nation had no energy for exploration. Russia was shut out from the family of Europe. It was indeed hardly in any sense a European country at all.

Struggles for a Seaboard

But Ivan IV desired to enter into the family of Europe. In that way alone he saw he could make his country great, and he determined to "open a window into Europe." To do that he knew he must have a seaboard. So he fought the Mongols on his southern borders and conquered Astrakan. Thus, by way of the Volga and the Caspian, he opened up a trade route to Persia and the East. But for a Baltic port he fought in vain, The Brothers of the Sword, indeed, were, dispersed, but Poland and Sweden remained masters of the Baltic shores. Not until a hundred and fifty years later, under a greater czar than Ivan, was Russia to obtain the coveted seaboard on the Baltic.

But although, through Teutonic jealousy, the Baltic was closed to their traders, the Russians had a seaboard to the north. The entrance to it lay indeed within the Arctic Circle, and for many months of the year it was closed by ice. But English sailors were busy seeking new passages to the East "by the high way of the seas," and while in search for a north-east passage to China they found Russia.

Very soon, by way of this icy northern route a brisk trade grew up between England and Russia. Dutch, Spanish, Italian, and French merchants followed them, but the English, who had been first in the field, kept the bulk of the trade.

Thus, in spite of the jealousy of Germans, Poles, and Swedes, "a window was opened into Europe." Had it not been for this jealousy Russia would have developed much faster than it did. But all these nations feared lest Russia should become powerful, and did their best to shut her out from the commerce, the learning, the industries, and the weapons of warfare of western Europe. It is even said that the king of Sweden threatened with death the English sailors and adventurers who tried to trade with Russia. So in her struggle towards civilization Russia was hindered and thwarted, and remained for long years to come what the Tartar domination had made it, an Asiatic Empire.

Yet, in spite of every hindrance Ivan the Terrible left his Empire stronger and more advanced than he had found it. He was a strange mixture of savagery and greatness. As a statesman he was far ahead of his times, and he understood the needs of his kingdom better than any man. But he was cruel and vicious, and had an ungovernable temper. An Englishman who lived in those days has described him as "a goodlie man of person . . . full of readie wisdom, cruell, bloudye, merciles." For the first fourteen years of his reign Ivan showed his "readie wisdom" well and wisely. It was towards the end of his life that he proved himself "bloudye" and "merciles" and earned his surname of the Terrible. Then he crushed the great nobles with a pitiless hand, massacring them and their families, and laying waste the land with brutal fury.

After the death of Ivan the Terrible Russia again fell on troublous times. His dynasty soon died out, and in 1613, after a great uprising of the people, Michael Romanoff who, through a female side of his family, traced his descent from Rurick, was chosen czar. He had no great talent or ability, but he was the first of the house which was to rule over Russia until the abdication of his descendant Nicholas in 1918.

THE RISE OF SWITZERLAND

IT was during the fight for the Empire between Lewis IV and Frederick the Handsome (see Chapter XXX) that the Swiss struggle for freedom began. From the eleventh century the land now known as Switzerland had been part of the Empire. As a nation it did not then exist, but was divided into cantons. One of these cantons was called Schwyz, and in time it gave its name to the whole country.

The mountaineers who lived in these cantons were a brave and freedom-loving people, but they paid a loyal, if somewhat shadowy, allegiance to the emperor. Now the Hapsburgs, who were dukes of Austria, tried to convert these cantons into a mere family possession. This the Swiss resisted with all their strength, and three forest cantons, Schwyz, Uri, and Unterwarden, formed themselves into a league for national protection and defence.

William Tell

Of the beginning of this resistance, in the early part of the fourteenth century, William Tell is the hero. Tell has been proved to the satisfaction of most people to be a myth. But the story, at least, illustrates how irksome the servile homage, demanded by a feudal overlord, had become to men who had grown to respect themselves, and had ceased to look upon themselves as mere chattels.

The first great battle for Swiss freedom was fought at Morgarten between the League and the Austrians in 1315. The Austrians were led by Leopold, duke of Austria, fighting in the interests of his brother Frederick. His army was filled with the flower of Austrian knighthood, but it went down before the untrained mountaineers fighting for freedom. This first great victory had two results. It checked the rule of Austria over the three forest states, and it bound them closer together.

Lewis was not ill-pleased to see the House of Austria thus defeated, and he rather favoured the League, which during his reign grew considerably stronger. What the Swiss fought for was not severance from the Empire, but freedom from the oppressions of the House of Austria. The dukes of Austria, however, were by no means minded to lose their power over these mountaineers and cowkeepers. So, save when they were too deeply engaged with schemes in other parts of the Empire, they carried on a fairly constant warfare against the Swiss.

These wars availed Austria little, while the Confederation grew constantly stronger. At length, seventy-one years after Morgarten, in the reign of Wenceslaus, the besotted son of Charles IV, the Austrians were again utterly defeated at the battle of Sempach. In this battle, as at the battle of Morgarten, they were again led by a Leopold of Austria, a nephew of the former duke.

Arnold von Winkelried

It was at Sempach that the patriot Arnold von Winkelried is said to have laid down his life for his country. The Austrian nobles stood a firm and glittering mass, and in spite of all their bravery the Swiss were unable to break through their lines. Seeing this Winkelried determined to force a way through.

"Comrades," he said, "I will make a way for you." Then spreading his arms wide and crying aloud, "Make way for Liberty," he ran upon the bristling spears, and gathering as many as he could to his breast, sank dying to the ground. The wall of steel was broken, and through the breach thus made the Swiss marched to victory.

Two years after Sempach the Swiss won another victory at Nafels. By these two battles the power of Austria over the Confederacy was shattered. The Hapsburgs resigned their claims, and signed a peace for seven years. This peace was renewed from time to time, and for many a long day the brave mountaineers were left to themselves, and gradually grew stronger as more towns and cantons joined the League.

In 1439 Albert, duke of Austria, was elected emperor. From that date until 1806, when Francis II resigned his empty title, in spite of a show of election, the title remained with hardly a break hereditary in the Hapsburg family, Charles V and Francis I being the only emperors not of the House of Austria.

Zurich and Austria

During the reign of Albert's son, Frederick III, the Swiss were involved in civil war. Zurich, one of the cantons, concluded a separate alliance with Austria. This caused such anger in the Confederacy that they made war against Zurich. The emperor then made an alliance with France, and in spite of the fact that France was still in the throes of the Hundred Years' War, obtained from him an army of thirty thousand soldiers under the Dauphin Louis. This army was little more than a rabble of hungry adventurers, but it was twice as large as the Swiss army, and at St. Jacob's, near 1444 Basle, the Swiss were defeated.

Yet although the Swiss lost the battle they had made such a brave fight that it counted as one more step towards freedom. The war continued, and five years later Zurich gave up its alliance with Austria and was again received into the Confederacy.

Twenty-six years after the battle of St. Jacob's the Swiss made an alliance with Louis XI, who, as Dauphin, had defeated them. Secretly encouraged by the wily Louis, they became embroiled in war with his great enemy Charles of Burgundy. In two great battles, one at Granson and one at Morat, they utterly defeated him. The following year Charles was killed in a battle near Nancy.

These victories welded the Confederates still more closely together, and from now onward they began to be looked upon as a nation, and received the name of Swiss.

This new nation was still in name part of the Empire, but it was, in fact, quite independent. The Swiss had not fought against the Empire but against the House of Austria. The emperors were now, however, continuously drawn from the Hapsburgs, and showed an inherited desire to subdue Switzerland. This the Swiss resisted.

They were now so strong that they had no need of protection from the Empire, which, indeed, was in no condition to give protection, and had itself become a feeble shadow. They were able, by their own authority, to keep the peace within their own borders, and they had no need to have the king's peace thrust upon them.

Yet the emperors still obstinately regarded the country as part of the Empire, and in 1499 the Emperor Maximilian I again tried to force the Swiss to acknowledge his sway and began a campaign against them.

But in this war he got little aid from the Empire as a whole, for most of the states regarded it as a purely Austrian quarrel. The Swiss, on the other hand, fought with the glorious courage which comes to a small nation fighting for its very existence against the overweening pride of militarism. And they won. After eight months of bitter struggle Maximilian was defeated and forced to conclude the Pease of Basle.

After this Switzerland was practically independent, but this independence was not openly acknowledged until the Peace of Westphalia in 1648.

The many victories which the Swiss had won over their powerful foes had gained for them a great reputation as fighters, and from the time of their wars with Charles the Bold onward all the rulers in Europe, but especially the French, became eager to have Swiss soldiers in their armies. In consequence, Switzerland became sort of a "market of men," and in almost every great campaign Swiss mercenaries were to be found fighting on one side or another. It was not until the nineteenth century that many of the cantons forbade foreign enlistment. Yet, strange to say, in spite of fighting thus on any side for which they were paid to fight, the Swiss kept their own nationality, and amid the broils of Europe the little republic has remained safe and intact.

In the reign of Frederick, under whom the Swiss practically secured their freedom, the Empire sank to its lowest. It was shorn of its dependencies, war raged everywhere throughout the land, the great princes each struggling to increase their power and wealth while the Empire was reduced to the last stage of beggary. Yet the lower the Empire sank the greater grew the arrogance of the Emperor, and Frederick took for his motto the letters A.E.I.O.U., which stood for the Latin Austria Est Imperare Orbi Universo, or in German, Alles Erdreich ist Oesterreich Unterthan.

But while the wearer of this proud motto sat upon the throne Constantinople fell before the Turks. They overran Europe, reaching even to the borders of Austria, and the emperor raised no finger to stay their course. It was left to the Poles and the Hungarians to sweep back the Moslem tide which threatened to overwhelm the Western even as it had overwhelmed the Eastern Empire.

While Frederick arrogantly proclaimed the subjection of all the realms of earth to Austria, dauntless adventurers were sailing unknown seas, revealing new and undreamed of lands. But Germany without unity or nationality had no part in these discoveries, and neither then nor later did she share the heritage of Europe in the New World.

Maximilian I

In 1493 Maximilian, the son of Frederick III, succeeded his father as emperor. He was the first who took the title of emperor without waiting to go to Rome to be crowned by the pope. Up to this time the German overlord had only been styled king of the Romans until crowned by the pope. But Italy was at this time full of war, and the journey to Rome was one of difficulty and danger. So in 1508 Maximilian announced that he intended to take the title of emperor.

The pope, Julius II, was anxious to have Maximilian on his side in his Italian wars, so he gave his consent. After this all the emperors took the title on their election, and only one (Charles V) went to Rome to be crowned.

In his own time Maximilian was one of the best loved of German emperors. Yet he never did anything for the Empire. He was constantly at war, and nearly always defeated.

He has been called the last of the knights, yet he did more than any other Continental ruler to kill knighthood, for he was one of the first to follow the example of England and organize foot soldiers for his army to take the place of the splendid but useless mounted knights.

He was vainglorious and vacillating, and succeeded in little. Yet through him great European complications were to arise. In 1477, long before he became emperor, he married Mary of Burgundy, the daughter of Charles the Bold, who fought the Swiss. Through her he became possessed of Burgundy and the Netherlands. When Maximilian became emperor he gave the government of the Netherlands to his son Philip. This son married Joanna, the daughter of Ferdinand and Isabella of Spain, and thus Spain and the Netherlands became united. All this had important results for Europe.

LIST OF EMPERORS

Rudolf I of Hapsburg,	1273-1291.
Albert I of Hapsburg,	1298-1308.
Henry VII of Luxemburg,	1308-1313.
Lewis IV of Bavaria,	1314-1347.
Frederick the Fair of Hapsburg,	1314-1330.
Charles IV of Luxemburg,	1347-1378.
Wenzel of Luxemburg,	1378-1400.
Rupert of the Palatinate,	1400-1410.
Sigismund of Luxemburg,	1410-1438.
Albert II of Hapsburg,	1438-1439.
Frederick III of Hapsburg,	1440-1493.
Maximilian I of Hapsburg,	1493-1519.

THE BEGINNING OF ITALIAN
UNITY SHATTERED

ALL the states of which we have so far heard had, by the end of the fifteenth century, passed through the formative stage. They had all consolidated into nationality except Germany, which was still a conglomeration of states, and Italy, which was yet without nationality, unity, or central government.

This was chiefly do to the efforts of Germany to impose German rule upon the Italians. Frederick II, who was Italian rather than German, was the last, and almost the only, German emperor who had in this any chance of success (see Chapter XXVII). He failed, and after him the emperors interfered little, and always with disastrous results, in the affairs of Italy.

Yet Italy found no peace, and until the middle of the fourteenth century it was torn by civil wars. Princely families rose and fell, while more than one despot schemed in vain to draw the whole country under his rule. The rival factions were still called Guelph and Ghibeline, but the real struggle was no longer between the pope and emperor. It was rather between feudalism and commerce, between inaction and progress.

Out of this welter of warfare there arose in Italy, towards the middle of the fifteenth century, five chief powers. Thy largest of these was the kingdom of Naples. This included the whole southern portion of the peninsula as well as the island of Sicily. Then, like a wedge across the centre of the peninsula lay the papal states. North of these were the republics of Florence and of Venice and the Duchy of Milan.

Florence and Venice were termed republics, but the rule in them, as in all Italian states, tended to despotism. And despotism brought in its train the usual crop of plots and murders. Yet, in spite of this tendency towards despotism Italy had made some advance towards freedom and nationality in that her despots were all Italian, and not imposed upon her by an alien power. Even Alfonso, king of Naples, a Spaniard by birth, was Italian in his sympathies.

The five states, moreover, had a common language, a common literature, and love of art, and through these there began to dawn among

152

them a feeling of common nationality. Thus in Italy it was through a love of learning and of art that the sense of nationality awoke, and not as in other nations through war and a necessity for combining against a common foe.

Politically, however, in the fifteenth century there were as yet no Italians. There were merely Venetians, Florentines, Genoese, Neapolitans, and so on. Still for a time there was a sort of peaceful federation among the five greatest states, and between the years 1447 and 1492 Italy was more free, and more at rest from foreign domination, than it had been for many generations. Had this time of peace been allowed to last, had the country been left free from pernicious alien interference, unity might have been attained much earlier.

As it was Italy was still centuries away from unity. It was still for centuries to be torn to pieces, and subjected to the tyranny of foreign princes.

In 1266 Charles of Anjou, on the invitation of the popes Urban IV and Clement VI, had taken possession of the kingdom of Naples, which included Sicily. The French domination was very irksome to the Sicilians, and in 1282 the rebellion known as the Sicilian Vespers broke out. The French were massacred wholesale, and driven from the island. Then the Sicilians called Peter of Aragon, who had married the daughter of Tancred (see Chapter XIV) to the throne.

After this the house of Anjou ruled in Naples, the house of Aragon in Sicily. But in 1435 the Angevin dynasty died outwith Joanna II, and the kingdom passed, not without bloodshed, to the king of Sicily, Alfonso of Aragon, surnamed the Magnanimous. Thus Spanish domination on the mainland was begun.

Charles VIII. The French in Italy

When Louis XI, king of France, died in 1483 he was succeeded by his son Charles VIII, a boy of thirteen. Charles was a throw-back into mediævalism. He was full of romantic ideas, sighing for picturesque wars and victories, and all the splendours of an outworn feudalism. As an Angevin he claimed the throne of Naples, and when invited to invade Italy by a would-be duke of Milan, Ludovico the Moor, he joyfully accepted.

Like a knight of old, he laid his lance in rest, and with banners waving in the breeze and trumpets sounding, he rode into Italy surrounded by all the pomp of a feudal army. Yet this apparently feudal pomp was purely theatrical. Charles, however much he wished it, could not turn back the hands of time, and in reality his army was mostly made up of mercenaries.

His progress was a pageant rather than a campaign, and without drawing a sword he passed through Italy to Naples. Alfonso fled at his coming, and almost without opposition Charles was crowned, assuming, besides that of King of Naples, the empty titles of Emperor of the East and King of Jerusalem.

But while in Naples Charles played at Empire, Ferdinand, King of Spain, Maximilian I, Emperor of Germany, together with some of the Italian princes (among them that same Duke of Milan who had invited him to invade Italy), joined in a league against him. Hurriedly then the pageant emperor beat a retreat. But at Fornova he found the armies of the allies barring the way. With the courage of desperation he faced his foes. The result was a bare victory for the French, but it secured their return to France.

Having reached his own land again in safety all recollection of his short-lived triumph in Italy seemed to pass from the mind of Charles, and he never renewed his claim to the throne of Naples.

At first sight this campaign seems of small importance. Charles had done little but ride through Italy and ride back again. But it had great results. It meant the discovery of Italy by the rest of Europe, and a French writer declares that this discovery of Italy had more effect on the sixteenth century than the discovery of America. With it began a long and disastrous interference of France in the affairs of Italy, an interference prejudicial alike to both countries. The folly of France, in thus wasting her energies in an unjust war of aggression, prevented her from taking a higher place among the nations of Europe, and shattered the beginning of Italian unity.

Rodrigo Borgia and Savonarola

Meanwhile, although the French were driven out of Italy, there was no peace for the unhappy land. The infamous Rodrigo Borgia was pope. He had taken the title of Alexander VI, and never had Italy more cause to be ashamed of her pontiff and her priesthood. For Alexander was one of the worst popes who ever sat upon the papal throne. Courteous, magnificent, and a great lover of art, he was yet wicked and cruel, and so greedy of wealth and power, both for himself and his family, that he cared not if he plunged the whole of Italy into war to gain his ends.

He cared nothing for his sacred office, and never did the Church sink so low as under his rule. But already the day of reform was dawning. In Florence a monk named Girolamo Savonarola raised his voice against the evil living of the great prince of the Church. He was austere as a Hebrew prophet, and spoke with such fierce eloquence that the pleasure-loving Florentines were shaken out of their careless paganism. At his bidding they made bonfires of their works of art, and all such "vanities"; they cast away their splendid garments of silk, their ornaments of gold, and dressed with the simplicity of monks and nuns.

Savonarola was a reformer before the Reformation. But he was not a reformer as we have come to understand the word. He preached not schism but righteousness, and to the day of his death he believed with all his heart in the teaching of the Church.

It was the coming of Charles VIII that brought Savonarola to the front in Italian politics. It seemed to him that Charles was the instrument of God's vengeance upon Italy for her sins. To resist him was to resist God, and out of his own enthusiasm he endowed the frivolous French monarch with all the attributes of a divine messenger and minster of justice. Yet, when the tyrant Piero de Medici had been expelled from Florence, it was Savonarola who persuaded Charles to move southward, and leave the republic in peace to reframe her constitution.

Savonarola took a great part in the reframing of this constitution, and for a time the Florentines followed him whither he led them with a passionate devotion. But if Savonarola saw in Charles Italy's great hope others regarded him and his army merely as barbarians, to be driven from the land as speedily as might be. Many of the northern states, therefore, joined with the king of Spain and the emperor in the League of Venice against France. Florence, however, under Savonarola's guidance, refused to join.

This refusal roused the wrath of the pope, for he, more than all the other princes, wanted to be rid of Charles. And as Savonarola would not yield, he swore his downfall. First, however, he bribed him with the promise of a cardinal's hat. Savonarola refused it scornfully. He would have no red hat, he said, save the red crown of a martyr.

As this pestilent friar would not hear reason Alexander VI excommunicated him. Gradually then troubles thickened about him. He lost influence, his beloved Florentines fell away from him, his enemies increased in number and power. At length he was seized and condemned to death for schism and heresy. On May 23, 1498, he was hanged, and his body was afterwards burned.

Savonarola was a great, pure-minded man, hating sin and loving with a great tenderness the sinful and the weak. Whether he was a perfect patriot can scarcely be decided without a perfect knowledge of the troublous times in which he lived. It was not possible for him to be a great reformer and a great politician at one and the same time. So, passionately earnest, fiercely righteous and noble-minded although he was, he failed. His chief failure, it may be, lay in that he trusted to outside aid, instead of bidding his people be strong in themselves. Yet for good or evil his spirit lived after him, and no one can think of the struggles of Italy at this time without taking Savonarola into account.

THE STRUGGLE BETWEEN FRANCE AND SPAIN FOR SUPREMACY IN ITALY

THE same year in which Savonarola was put to death Louis XII succeeded Charles VIII upon the throne of France. Under him the history of France is little more than the history of Italian campaigns. For Louis XII laid claim not only to Naples but to the Duchy of Milan. Warned, however, by the fate of Charles VIII, before entering upon his campaign he arranged for the concurrence of the other chief rulers in Europe.

Louis was supported by the pope, who was not unwilling to increase the papal states at the expense of the rest of Italy, and with little trouble he conquered Milan, and made it a province of France. Then he turned his thoughts to Naples. Here he feared the opposition of Spain, so he made an alliance with Ferdinand, King of Spain, who promised him aid in return for a share of the spoils.

The conquest of Naples was an easy matter, but when it was accomplished the royal robbers quarrelled over the division of the spoil. Louis found that he had been merely Ferdinand's cat's-paw and was obliged to resign to him the whole of Naples, and content himself with Milan, which he had conquered without his aid.

While Louis and Ferdinand were quarrelling, the pope, Alexander VI, used them in turn for his own ends. He cared not at all for Italy but desired to increase the papal states in the hope of bequeathing them to his cruel and unscrupulous son, Cæsar Borgia. So while the north and the south of the peninsula were given over to foreigners, he tried to make a solid kingdom in the centre.

Alexander seemed to be succeeding admirably when he suddenly died. Then all the states which he had gathered with such guile and wile reverted to the Church, and not to Borgia, who soon fell from power and shortly left Italy.

Julius II and the Papal States

The next pope, Julius II, set himself also to strengthen the papal states. He did this, however, to increase the power of the Church rather than that of his own family.

He was a statesman and a soldier more than a pastor, and was eager to drive the barbarians out of Italy. But he wanted to be sure that when they were gone the papal states would be stronger than any other state in Italy.

To secure this he desired to crush Venice first. So in 1508 he persuaded the Emperor Maximilian, Louis XII of France, and Ferdinand of Spain to join him in the League of Cambray against Venice. In the ensuing war Louis was again merely a cat's-paw, and when with his help Venice was sufficiently crushed, the pope made peace with the republic. He then formed a new League called the Holy League. This was much the same as the League of Cambray, only now the place of France was taken by Venice, and King Henry VIII of England was also included. The armies of this League were soon turned against Louis, and the French were driven beyond the Alps.

Julius would now willingly have turned the Spaniards out of Italy also. But with this he was not so successful, and in 1513 he died, leaving them still strongly entrenched in the south. Louis also did not lightly give up his ambitions; and shortly after the death of Julius he became reconciled to the Venetians, and with their aid once more made an effort to conquer Milan. But the campaign ended in disaster, and the French were once more driven from Italy.

Under these repeated defeats France seemed crushed, and it appeared to her many enemies the moment to attack her. The Swiss invaded the east, Spaniards threatened the south, while Henry VIII landed with twenty thousand men at Calais. He was soon joined by the Emperor Maximilian, and the French were defeated at the battle of Guinegate.

Louis was now utterly weary of the wars which had filled his reign. He longed for peace, and made overtures to the pope. Fortunately for France Leo X had none of the war-like ambitions of Julius or Alexander, and he became reconciled. By degrees the League was dissolved, and peace made with its various members.

In 1515 Louis XII died. In spite of the many foreign wars during his reign, and that of Charles VIII, France had progressed. For the wars for the most part had been carried on without her borders, and the nobles had no longer the right of private war wherewith to disturb the public peace. Feudalism had disappeared, and the feudal lords had been transformed into courtiers. The king's authority was greater than it had ever been, and he was more able to enforce obedience to his will. And in the short periods when he was not absorbed in his wars of aggression, Louis had used his power well. He had protected the people, encouraged agriculture and commerce, so that the general wealth of the nation was increased.

Francis I and Charles V

Francis I succeeded Louis XII, and he, too, was bitten with desire of conquest in Italy, and almost at once began to make preparations for an invasion. By the victory of Marignano he regained Milan. It was, however, now no longer a question of conquering the Italians, but of fighting the Spaniards. It was, in fact, a Franco-Spanish war fought in Italy, and in 1525 at Pavia Francis was utterly defeated. He lost everything which France claimed in Italy, and was himself taken prisoner, and Italy became the prey of Spain.

Before this a great change had taken place in the balance of power in Europe. For in 1516 Ferdinand of Spain died. He was succeeded by his grandson Charles, the son of his daughter Joanna. Through her Charles inherited all Spain, and all the Spanish conquests in Italy, as well as the vast Empire which Spain now claimed in the New World.

In 1519 the Emperor Maximilian died. Charles was also his grandson, his father being Philip, the son of Maximilian and Mary of Burgundy. From his grandfather Maximilian he inherited all the Austrian possessions of the Hapsburgs; from his grandmother Mary he inherited the Netherlands, comprising roughly the present kingdoms of Holland and Belgium.

Added to this Charles was elected emperor with the title of Charles V. So apart from his actual possessions he was suzerain of the German states and claimed with the title of emperor a vague lordship over the whole of Italy. He held Europe, it was said, by the four corners; and in days when wars of aggression were the right of the strong, the accumulation of so much power in the hands of one man threatened the freedom and peace of the continent.

To France especially his power seemed a menace. For France was enclosed by his possessions save where the sea laid her open to attack by her ancient enemy England. It was hardly wonderful then that France should endeavour to lessen his power and dispute his possession of Italy. But besides this real menace there was personal enmity between Francis I and Charles. For Francis I had hoped to be chosen emperor; that he was not was a bitter disappointment to him, and throughout the rest of his life he kept a jealous wrath against Charles. He was constantly at war with him, and Italy was the battle-field upon which these wars were fought.

But the defeat of the French at Pavia and the captivity of their king brought no peace to Italy. As emperor, Charles claimed a vague suzerainty over the whole of Italy, but it was rather by right of conquest and as king of Spain that he enforced his claim. In resisting it the country was filled with confusion, every petty prince struggling for his own advantage. Thirty thousand marauding imperial troops, half German, half Spanish, seized and sacked Rome. Turkish pirates harried the coasts, carrying off both men and women to be sold into slavery, while their French allies devasted the land.

But in the end Spain triumphed. Italy was carved into states and parcelled out as Spain desired, her princes obeyed Spain's will. Then for more than two hundred and fifty years Italy could hardly be said to have a history of her own. She was tossed about from one ruler to another, and her fair plains were the battle-fields for quarrels not her own.

THE RENAISSANCE

WE use the word Renaissance to indicate the term of years between the Middle Ages and modern times. No exact dates are possible. Roughly, it began in Italy towards the end of the fourteenth century, with the revival of learning there, and gradually spread to the rest of Europe.

The word Renaissance is also used to mean, not merely the term of years between mediæval and modern times, but the new manner in which men began at this period to look at life, in the way of moral conduct and of learning. It was in one aspect a revolt of man against the accepted order of things, an awakening in man of the desire to think his own thoughts and to live his own life. It was a many-sided and complicated movement, touching and transforming all life. It was an advance; but in order to make this advance men retired backward to the learning of the ancients.

During the years when nations had been forming, when the business of life was war, learning had been neglected. Greek was a forgotten language in Western Europe. Plato was unknown, Homer and Aristotle known only in Latin translations. The books of these and other great writers might indeed be found in libraries. But they lay there unopened, for no one could read them, and there were neither dictionaries nor grammars from which the language might be learned. Only in Constantinople, the eastern outpost of Christian Europe, did the old learning survive.

Italy and the Humanists

As the Turks encroached upon the Grecian Empire many Greeks sought new homes in Italy. There they were warmly welcomed by the young writers of the day, such as Petrarch and Boccaccio. Petrarch, indeed, could never learn Greek at all, Boccaccio never learned it thoroughly, yet they were the forerunners of the Renaissance. They set Italy on the right road, and awoke a desire in the heart of the Italians for the beauties of the old Greek learning and culture.

This return to Greek and Greek art was a revolt against priestly authority and a return to nature. The whole treasure, therefore, of Greek and Latin literature which was now discovered, came to be called the

Humanities—litteræ humaniores. The men who advanced the movement came to be called the Humanists, and Petrarch, it has been said, was the first of the Humanists.

Italy had shown itself ready to imbibe Greek learning and Greek art. So it was naturally to Italy that most of the learned fled for refuge, when in 1453 Constantinople was taken by the Turks. These refugees brought with them their books and pictures as well as their love of art and learning. They found, as it were, the soil ready for them, and there the new-old learning took fresh root and blossomed.

Soon the fame of this learning spread abroad. It was not unhelped by war. For invading armies came. Italy was crushed between the upper and nether millstones of warring princes. Yet because of her art and learning she was not wholly crushed. Through them she conquered the conquerors, and scholars came from every part of Europe to sit at the feet of her learned doctors. Returning home they carried to the universities of France, Germany, and England perfect literary models, and opened treasures of long-forgotten knowledge to them.

From Italy, too, there spread a new love of art. Francis I carried back to France with him pictures by great artists such as Michael Angelo, Raphael, and Leonardo da Vinci. He induced Leonardo and other great artists to come to France, there to build for him splendid castles and churches. Taught by his example great architects soon arose in Spain and the Netherlands. To all the nations of Europe indeed there came a new conception of building. As art and learning began to fill a part of life which had hitherto been given only to war, the gloomy feudal castles began to disappear and noble pleasure houses took their place.

In this connection the discovery of gunpowder changed the world enormously. There has been much discussion as to who first discovered it in Europe. But whether it was a German monk, Berthold Schwartz, or Roger Bacon, in any case it began to be used in the middle of the fourteenth century. Its use changed the art of war, and struck a fatal blow at feudalism and chivalry. Henceforth the knight on horseback was of little use in the field. His prowess with lance and sword availed him little, when death could be dealt from a distance, leaving him never a chance of a hand-to-hand fight with his equals. The cloth-yard arrows of the English archer had wounded him sorely, the leaden bullet of the low-born arquebusier was his death-blow.

As the knowledge of the power of gunpowder increased, the stone-battlemented castles of the nobles were rendered useless as places of refuge. For walls strong enough to resist the heaviest of battering-rams crumbled before cannon-balls. And the consciousness that these formidable piles were useless helped the spread of gracious architecture.

Gunpowder was a great reformer and leveller, but printing was a greater, and it did more than anything else to encourage the spread of learning. The art had been known to the Chinese long before it was invented in Europe, and, as with gunpowder, there is doubt as to the first European discoverer. It may have been Janszoon Coster of Haarlem who first discovered it, or it may have been Johan Gutenberg of Mainz. But whoever discovered it, it came into use about the middle of the fifteenth century.

The art very quickly spread through Italy, France, and the Netherlands, and thence was brought by Caxton to England. By the end of the century printing-presses were busy in every country in Europe.

Nothing changed the world so much as this invention. Without it the new learning might have remained the privilege of the few. Without it man's dawning sense of individuality might never have come to the full light of day. As it was, printing made a gift of learning to the many. At the very outset, too, its influence was increased by the discovery of new, cheap ways of making paper. So with a quickness never surpassed, books, from being the luxury of the few, became the everyday necessity of all.

The New World

In the fifteenth century, in these and many other ways, the old world changed rapidly. Then, as if that were not enough, men discovered a new world. Christopher Columbus showed the way across the Atlantic. Vasco da Gama doubled the Cape of Good Hope. Magellan's expedition sailed round the world. In the wake of Columbus many other great sailors followed, until it was at length established beyond a doubt that his first voyage had led him not to India, as he believed, but to the shores of a mighty, and till then undreamed of, continent.

All these voyages made plain several matters. They made plain the fact that the world was round, that it was inhabited on the other side, that it was much larger than had been supposed. Now the first two facts

163

revealed were "heresy." The Church had taught that the world was flat or concave. To believe in the Antipodes and to believe that the Antipodes were inhabited was pronounced sinful. For had not the Apostles been commanded to go forth to preach the Gospel to the whole world? They never went to the Antipodes. Therefore, there was no such place.

But the daring sailors who sailed forth now almost daily, had proved beyond all possible contradiction that the world was round, and that the Antipodes were inhabited. This was a shock not only to men's preconceived ideas of the world's geography but to their faith. The Church was proved wrong in one dogma, might it not, they asked themselves, be wrong in others? Thus the discovery of the New World encouraged men to think for themselves, and decide for themselves in matters of religion.

The discovery of the New World opened a crack for doubt. It also, as it were, changed the axis of the old world. Henceforth the Mediterranean was no longer the centre of trade and commerce. In the twelfth and thirteenth centuries almost the entire trade and commerce of Europe had been in the hands of the Italians. They were very often all called Lombards (hence Lombard Street in London). They were not only the merchants but the bankers, manufacturers, and carriers for Europe. Upon this trade cities such as Venice grew great and splendid.

With the discovery of America this was changed. Trade drifted away from Italy and the Mediterranean ports to those countries opening upon the Atlantic. Many Italian ports were utterly ruined, many others fell from splendour to insignificance, merely because their geographical position as regards the New World, and the new ways to the old world, was disadvantageous.

The New World became the heritage of the people who united a good geographical position with grit, daring, and love of adventure. Spain, Portugal, England, France, and the Netherlands all shared the good geographical position, and all started fair in the race. But in the end Britain out-distanced all rivals. Germany, because of geographical position and want of political unity, took no part in it whatever, and has never since been able to make up for lost opportunities in the beginning. Italy, tied to the wheels of German ambition, shared her misfortune.

THE NEW ASTRONOMY

Nicolas Copernicus

WITH the discovery of the New World the axis of the old world was changed. With the spread of individual thought men's ideas of the entire universe changed also. The old astronomy had taught that the earth was the centre of the universe, and that the sun and all the planets revolved round it in a proper and humble manner.

Now Nicolas Copernicus, a Polish astronomer, published a book in which he explained that the sun, and not the earth, was the centre of the universe, and that the earth revolved round the sun like any other planet. This was another shock to man's faith. Such an idea was considered by the Church as heretical and contrary to Scripture. Had not Joshua commanded the sun to stand still? And had not the sun obeyed him?

To the ignorant theologians of the day it seemed that Copernicus was attacking the very foundations of religion. To them he was not an eager seeker after truth but a wicked man who must be silenced and punished for his wickedness. Copernicus escaped any persecution, as he died almost as soon as his book was published. His theory, however, did not die with him. Others carried on his work, just as others had carried on that of Columbus. They were the men, it had been said, who did more than any others to alter the mental attitude of humanity. Yet it was nearly a hundred years after the death of Copernicus that Galileo Galilei, an Italian astronomer, began openly to spread his teaching.

Galileo

Then once again the blind defenders of orthodoxy were in arms, and Galileo was threatened with the Inquisition, and forbidden to teach a theory which was "expressly contrary to Holy Scripture." He promised obedience, and was left in peace. But sixteen years later he forgot his promise, and wrote a book in which he supported the teaching of Copernicus.

At once the thunders of the Church were launched against him. He was by this time an old man of seventy. But that did not save him from

165

torture and imprisonment, and under the threat of death by fire his courage gave way, and he retracted. He acknowledged his errors, and declared that the earth was stationary. But, it is said, that as he rose from his knees after making his confession, he was heard to murmur, "Yet still it moves."

This recantation saved Galileo from death. He was, however, condemned to imprisonment during the pleasure of the Inquisition. But after a short time he was practically released, and allowed to live in his own house not far from Florence. Here, eight years later, he died, still nominally the prisoner of the Church.

But in spite of suppression and persecution the world moved on. The inquiring spirit of man once awakened could not be put to sleep again. An intense desire to know all that there was to know increased daily.

Giordano Bruno

One of the great leaders in this fight for liberty of thought and speech was Giordano Bruno, a Neapolitan monk. Persecuted and hunted from place to place, he was at last seized by the Inquisition, and after eight years' imprisonment was burned as a heretic.

"The earth," he said, "only holds her high rank among the stars by usurpation. It is time to dethrone her. Let this not dispirit man as if he thought himself forsaken by God. For if God is everywhere, if there is in truth an unnumbered host of stars and suns, what matters the vain distinction between the heaven and the earth? Dwellers in a star, are we not included in the celestial plains set at the very gates of Heaven?

Sayings such as these cost Bruno his life. Not unworthily has he been named "a hero of thought." He dared to break the bonds of "authority," to think for himself, and follow truth even to death.

As can be seen the new birth was accomplished only through much pain. The new day dawned on Europe slowly and stormily. But in spite of the hindering hand of superstition, in spite of dark dungeons and the rack, in spite of the stake and its cruel fires, the movement increased until at length the old order vanished, and the new took its place all over Western Europe. In every country, on all subjects, men fought for and won the right of private judgment, the right of individual freedom.

THE BEGINNING OF THE REFORMATION

EVERYTHING in the Renaissance did not make for good. It led towards freedom, but it also led towards godlessness and licence. But born of the same desire for truth, led by the same spirit of liberty, helped by the printing-press, even as the new learning was helped, another movement grew and spread. This was the Reformation.

The Reformation was not a revolt against the Renaissance but its natural accompaniment. They acted and re-acted upon each other. In everything men had begun to think for themselves. By new discoveries on the earth and in the heavens old beliefs had been shaken. It was not wonderful then that men should claim the right of freedom in religious thought as in all others.

Early Reformers

As the Renaissance had its forerunners, so also had the Reformation. At the beginning of the thirteenth century the Albigenses in the south of France had been crushed out of existence because they dared to worship God in their own way. In the middle of the fourteenth century in England John Wycliffe had preached against the doctrines of the Church, and had made the first translation of the Bible into English. He was persecuted but not silenced, and after his death his followers, the Lollards, continued to teach and preach until they were suppressed by force.

Wycliffe's teaching, however, was not killed, and it spread over Europe even as far as Bohemia. Here in the beginning of the fifteenth century John Huss began to preach his doctrines. He was burned at the stake, a crusade was declared against his followers, and for fifteen years they were hunted and persecuted.

But in the end these and other movements like them had all been crushed. None of them had the aid of the printing-press, therefore they remained more or less local, and left little impression on the world as a whole.

In spite of these occasional risings against its authority, the

167

pretension of the Church increased as time went on, until the pope claimed absolute authority over every country and every king, in secular as well as in spiritual matters. Kings, said the pope, in effect, could reign only by his will and favour. And if any displeased him he claimed the right of deposing him, and of giving his lands to another.

But as in each country the sense of nationality and the royal power grew greater, both kings and people began to chafe at this foreign interference. As the papacy became less spiritual and more and more secular, as the pope himself became less and less a pastor and more and more a ruling prince and warrior, this dissatisfaction increased. Kings grudged more and more the constant stream of gold which, flowing from their countries in the shape of tithes and other ecclesiastical fees, went, not to spread the Gospel of Christ, but to swell the exchequer of the pope as a temporal prince and possible political enemy.

On the political side, then, the world was ready to break with the pope. On the religious side it was also ready. For there came the new learning and the printing-press. Bibles were soon sown broadcast in the tongues of every nation in Europe. Men were no longer content to be told that such and such a doctrine was taught by the Church; they wanted to know why and upon what grounds the Church taught its doctrines. The Reformation was thus both a political and a religious movement. For in the Middle Ages Church and state had become so bound together that it could not be otherwise.

More than any other land Germany had felt the power of the pope. Because of the fatal connection between the Holy Roman Empire and the Holy See it had been kept from nationality, and had remained a collection of states great and small, held together by the slightest of bonds. Now, more than any other land, it was ready for revolt. The gunpowder was ready, the train was laid; it needed but a spark to fire it. The spark which caused the explosion was the sale of Indulgences.

The Sale of Indulgences

An Indulgence meant that by paying a sum of money a man could buy forgiveness of any sin he had committed. The selling of them was no new thing. It was closely connected with the practice of doing penance, many people preferring to pay money than do penance in other ways. But in early days no Indulgence had been given except upon the promise of repentance. By the end of the fifteenth century the sale of them had become a scandal. The most vile and wicked, who had neither the desire nor the intention of repentance, could buy them freely.

When an Indulgence seller set forth upon his rounds he did so in splendour, with a gay train of followers. Coming to a city he entered it with pomp. The Bull declaring the Indulgence was carried on a cushion of cloth of gold or of crimson velvet. Priests swinging censers and carrying lighted candles and banners followed after, and thus to the sound of chants and songs, and the ringing of joy bells, the procession passed along the streets to the church.

Here, before the altar, the vendor spread forth his wares, and declaring that the gates of heaven were open, invited the people to come and buy. When Leo X became pope he found his exchequer almost empty. He needed money sorely for his many projects, among them the building of St. Peter's at Rome. To get the money he fell back upon the fruitful expedient of selling Indulgences.

Martin Luther

The man who had charge of their sale in Germany was a Dominican monk named John Tetzel. He was vulgar and blasphemous. He cried his wares in the church like a cheap-jack in the market-place, making unseemly jokes by the way. This manner of selling Indulgences shocked many people who before had found no harm in the custom. Among these was the monk Martin Luther.

Luther was the son of a poor miner, and his childhood had been one of bitter poverty. But poor although he was, Hans Luther had managed to send his son to school and afterwards to the university of Erfurt, at that time the most famous in Germany.

His son repaid him by working hard, and it seemed as if he had a great career before him, when suddenly he threw all his brilliant prospects to the winds and became a monk. Martin took this step, he said, to save his soul. For he was one of those who had begun to think for themselves on matters of religion, and his thoughts had thrown him into an anguish of doubt. In time, however, he found some sort of peace, and when Tetzel came to Germany he was teacher of theology in the university of Wittenberg.

For various reasons many of the rulers in Germany disliked the selling of Indulgences, and the Elector of Saxony had forbidden Tetzel to enter his dominions. But Tetzel would not willingly forgo the harvest of gold which might be gleaned from Saxony. So, without actually entering its borders he came as near to them as he could, and set up his booth in Magdeburg. And as he had foreseen, many people crossed the frontiers to buy Indulgences.

At this Luther's heart was filled with sorrow and indignation. He could not but feel that these poor people were being deceived and exploited. At length he wrote out, in Latin, ninety-five theses, or articles, against the sale of Indulgences, and on November 1, 1517, he nailed them to the door of the castle church at Wittenberg. The chief idea in these theses was "that by true sorrow and repentance only, and not by payment of money, forgiveness of sins can be won."

REFORMATION PERIOD: GERMANY

WHEN Luther nailed his theses to the door of Wittenberg Church he had no idea of what a great thing he did. He had no idea that he had begun a vast world-shaking movement. He had merely, in the fashion of the day, invited any who liked to debate the matter in public with him. But soon all Germany rang with his challenge. For the theses said openly and clearly what many had thought in secret yet dared not give voice to. They were quickly translated into German and sown broadcast throughout the land. From Germany they spread all over Europe, until all Europe was filled with disputations.

At first the pope thought little of the matter, and looked upon it as a mere monkish squabble. But soon he saw that it was more than that, and he issued a Bull of excommunication against Luther. By this time, however, Luther had become aware of what a great mass of opinion he had on his side. And instead of trembling at the pope's wrath, he publicly burned the Bull.

Charles V

Eighteen months before this the Emperor Maximilian had died, and after much intriguing his grandson Charles had been chosen emperor. As emperor his rule was so widespread that it is hardly an exaggeration to say that the future of the Reformation was in his hands. And so far as European history is concerned the chief point of interest in his reign is his attitude towards the movement.

The very extent of Charles V's dominions saved the Reformation. For at the beginning of his reign as emperor, he was so much occupied with the complicated politics of his varied possessions, that he could not give his whole mind to the suppression of heresy in Germany.

Not till eighteen months after his election as emperor, more than three years after Luther had nailed his theses to the door of the castle church at Wittenberg, did Charles pay his first visit to his German dominions. There in January 1521 he held his first Diet at Worms. And to this Diet Luther was summoned to answer for his heresy.

During the three years which had passed since his first bold deed, Luther had become strengthened in his convictions. Now he refused to retract anything that he had said. So the Ban of the Empire was pronounced against him. Henceforth he might be hunted or slain like a beast of prey, and his books were ordered to be confiscated and burned.

Excommunication and Ban alike fell harmless. Luther had now so many powerful friends that none dared to lay hands upon him, and his books were openly bought and sold in far greater numbers than before.

Charles was a Catholic not from conviction but from heredity. The religious aspect of the Protestant revolt interested him not at all. The political aspect interested him much. He desired to make sure of the pope's help against his arch enemy Francis I in his Italian wars, and by condemning Luther he procured this help. But he also produced war in his German domains.

For, condemned by the pope and the emperor although he might be, not only many of the German people but many of the German princes supported Luther. Had the emperor's interests been undivided he would have crushed these Protestant princes with an iron hand. But as it was he dared not. For he had two great enemies, the French and the Turks. The Turks were constantly threatening his Hapsburg possessions, the French were constantly opposing him in Italy. To keep these two enemies in check Charles had need of German help.

Protestants

So in spite of all efforts against it the heresy spread. At length, however, the Diet met at Spires, and passed a decree forbidding any change of religion, and commanding mass to be said in all churches. Against this decree the Protestant princes issued a protest. And from this all those who then, or later, broke away from the Church of Rome, received the name of Protestants.

During all this time Charles had not again visited Germany, for the difficulties of his Spanish dominions kept him in Spain. But in 1530, finding himself at peace for the moment, he attended the Diet of Augsburg prepared to force his will upon the Protestants. The Protestant princes, however, refused to he coerced, and Melanethon, Luther's gentle and wise friend, drew up a Protestant Creed, and laid it before the Diet. From this it

172

is called the Confession of Augsburg, and is still the accepted Creed of the Lutheran Church.

The Protestant leaders now, too, fearing that Charles would try to enforce his will by arms, banded themselves into the Schmalkald League, and prepared to resist force by force. But for the time Charles forbore to coerce them. For the Turks besieged Vienna, and he had need of the support of the Protestant as well of the Catholic princes to guard his possessions. In order to gain this help he signed the religious Peace of Nuremberg. By this Protestants were granted full freedom to worship God as they would, until a General Council should be called to discuss and settle the matter.

Then, having defeated the Turks, Charles once more left Germany, to turn his sword against his other great enemy, Francis I. Between 1521 and 1544 Charles fought at least four distinct wars against Francis I for the possession of Italy. Again and again Francis was defeated. He signed treaties and truces, and broke them; he was taken prisoner and released; and finally, to the horror of Europe, he allied himself with the infidel Turk against the emperor. But even this did not save him from defeat, and at length the long struggle came to an end in 1544 with the Treaty of Crespy. This treaty left Francis little better off as regards Italy than he had been at the beginning of his reign, it also bound him to aid in the suppression of heresy.

The following year Charles signed a long truce with the Turks, and being thus free of his two chief enemies, he set out for Germany, determined to crush the Schmalkald League, and force all Germany to return to the old religion.

In 1546 the Schmalkald War broke out. At first Charles was successful, and it seemed as if at last he would be able to enforce his will on Germany. He had gained his early successes by the help of Maurice, duke of Saxony. But in the hour of his triumph Maurice turned against him; the war ended in disaster for Charles, and he was obliged to give up his design of forcing all Germany to think alike on matters of religion.

By the religious Peace of Augsburg in 1555 a religious toleration of a very limited kind was established. It gave to the ruler of each state power to decide what should be the religion of its people, and power to do as he liked with those who refused to conform to his religion. Thus the great revolt which had been awakened by the blows of Luther's hammer came to an end. The emperor and the pope had lost, and had been forced to give up their claim to be the keepers of the general conscience of mankind. But the people had not won. They had merely changed masters. Their princes were to be the keepers of their conscience, they were to be bishops as well as rulers. This was no real settlement. The strife was only ended for a time; later it was to break out more seriously than before.

The Abdication of Charles V

While the Peace of Augsburg was being concluded Charles V abdicated. He tried, but tried in vain, to make the electors choose his son Philip as emperor. They refused, and elected his brother Ferdinand instead. So to Philip Charles could only bequeath the Netherlands, the Italian provinces, and Spain, with all her vast possessions in America.

That Charles was able to leave the Italian provinces and the Netherlands to Philip without question is a signal proof of the ascendency of Spain in Europe at this time. For Italy had always been looked upon as a part of the Empire. Throughout centuries streams of German blood had been shed to acquire and hold it. But Charles, disregarding the fact that he had made his conquests by German aid, claimed Italy by right of conquest, and not by right of the ancient imperial claim. And as a Spanish possession he left the country to his son Philip.

The loss of Italy to the Empire was merely imaginary. It was, indeed, no real loss but a gain. A very real loss, and one which was to be felt in modern times, was the loss of the Netherlands. For centuries the northern part of the Netherlands, that part which is now Holland, had been included in the Empire. Now, by the will of Charles, it was severed from it without question or protest. And to this day the great German river, the Rhine, flows to the sea through a foreign country. Thus Charles V sowed the seeds of future warfare.

REFORMATION PERIOD SWITZERLAND
AND FRANCE

VERY quickly the new religion spread to other lands. Yet, save that it was Luther who, with unconscious courage, first showed the way, the Reformation in other countries had little connection with that of Germany.

In Switzerland the Reformation was led by Ulrich Zwingli. At this time the position of Switzerland was different from that of any other country in Europe. It had wrung itself free from the Empire and from the house of Austria, but it had not yet become a consolidated nation. Each of the thirteen cantons of which it was now composed had its own government, these governments varying considerably one from the other. There was thus not even the shadow of a central government, such as Germany had through the emperor, or Italy through the pope. They had not even a common language.

But in fact Switzerland was far more united than either Germany or Italy. Each canton was independent, yet each was a member of a federal league. They used a common flag, a white cross on a red ground, and a common motto, "Each for all, and all for each."

Since their war of independence the Swiss had had few wars of their own. Yet in nearly all the wars of Europe the Swiss took part, even at times a decisive part. For since their victorious struggle the Swiss had earned the reputation of being the best foot soldiers in Europe. And when by degrees paid soldiery took the place of feudal armies, warring kings and princes were eager to hire Swiss soldiery to fight for them. The sense of nationality was still feeble; one nation had as yet little sense of another nation's rights. It shocked none to find the men who had won their own liberty selling their swords and fighting a tyrant's battles.

The pope was one of the chief hirers of Swiss soldiery, and besides fighting in his army they formed his bodyguard, so that intercourse between Rome and Switzerland was constant. But this intercourse was purely commercial, and so far as religion was concerned Switzerland was singularly free from papal interference.

The Swiss Reformation began in the canton of Zurich, and soon spread to Berne. It began as in Germany with an attack on the sale of Indulgences. But although the movement spread rapidly, many in the Forest Cantons clung to the Romish faith. Soon the controversy between the two parties became so bitter that it led to civil war.

In 1531 the battle of Kappel was fought, in which the Protestants were defeated and Zwingli himself killed. After this a treaty was drawn up between the cantons, which left each free to settle its own religious matters.

John Calvin

Now that Zwingli was dead John Calvin became the leader of the Reformation in Switzerland, and Geneva took the place of Zurich as the centre of the movement. Calvin was a young Frenchman who had become a Protestant, and had been forced to flee from France to escape persecution. After Luther he was the greatest of the reformers, and his influence was far more wide reaching. The French Protestants and the English Puritans alike looked to him as their guide. John Knox was his follower, and taught his doctrine to the Scottish people, and the Pilgrim Fathers carried it across the Atlantic to the New World.

Calvin was himself a scholar, and he gathered many other scholars to Geneva, making it the stronghold of Protestantism and the centre of its teaching. It was from Geneva that the first trained teachers and pastors went forth to teach and preach the new faith. But the doctrine they taught was cold and narrow. For Calvin, although a learned man, was harsh and severe. He had none of the human kindliness of Luther, nor the open-mindedness of Zwingli.

Persecution of Protestants in France

In France the new religion met with terrible opposition. Yet there it was never a national movement, the Protestants always representing a minority, although a strong one. One reason for this was that the movement was not so much with them a political revolt against secular interference by the Pope as it was with other peoples. For ever since the "Babylonish Captivity," when the popes had been more or less subject to the French king, France had been more free than other nations from papal interference, and the headship of the French Church had belonged more to the French king than to the pope. So it came about that not being a

176

national movement, in time opposition and persecution were able practically to wipe out the Protestants of France.

By the Treaty of Crespy Francis I had bound himself to crush heresy within his dominions. Far less than Charles V had he himself any religious convictions, and was personally inclined to tolerance. But his complicated alliances drove him into many inconsistencies. So while he had not hesitated to ally himself with the Protestant princes of Germany against his enemy Charles, and even with the infidel Turk, to ingratiate himself with the pope he entered upon a cruel persecution of the Protestants of Provence.

These unoffending, devout, and loyal people were denounced as heretics and barbarously slaughtered. Neither age nor sex was respected, and three thousand men, women, and children were put to death. Others were sent to the galleys, and their villages laid in ruins.

In 1547 Francis died. Throughout his reign he had been stable in one thing—in his hatred of the house of Austria. In that he had shown wisdom. For the menace of Austria was a menace to all Europe, and not to France alone. In combating the desire for world dominion Francis had, in a sense, fought for Europe. He left France, moreover, actually increased in territory, stronger and more compact than before. He left her also more beautiful and advanced in culture. For he was the patron of both artists and men of letters, and many of the splendid castles which are still the glory of the Loire valley date from his reign.

Francis was succeeded by his son Henry II. He was a mediocre and feeble prince, and allowed himself to be guided by ambitious counsellors, chief among them the Guises.

Before long he was in league once more with the Protestant princes of Germany against his father's old enemy Charles. But now fortune had forsaken Charles, and from the walls of Metz he retired beaten.

During this reign the Reformation made great progress in France. Men high in office, and even princes of the royal blood, joined the movement. Growing bolder in consequence, many who formerly had only worshipped in secret openly confessed their adherence to the new faith, and in 1555 the first Protestant church was established in Paris.

Henry looked upon the spread of the new faith with fear and anger, and once more persecutions began. But these persecutions only made the Protestants cling more firmly to their faith.

REFORMATION PERIOD—
ENGLAND AND SCANDINAVIA

IN England the Reformation ran a different course from that in France or Germany. In these countries Protestantism spread in spite of the strenuous opposition of the rulers. In England it was aided by the ruler, King Henry VIII.

When Martin Luther first published his theses Henry VIII denounced him loudly, and as loudly upheld the headship of the pope. He even wrote a book called "The Defence of the Seven Sacraments," a copy of which, sumptuously bound, he sent to the pope. In return, Leo X bestowed upon him the title of Defender of the Faith.

A few years after this Henry desired to divorce his wife Katharine of Aragon, in order to marry Anne Boleyn. He professed a fear that he had sinned against heaven in marrying Katharine at all, as she was the widow of his elder brother Arthur, and he asked the pope, now Clement VII, to grant him a divorce.

Now Katharine was the daughter of Ferdinand and Isabella of Spain, and the aunt of the Emperor Charles V. So Henry's demand placed Clement in a difficult position. If he refused to grant Henry's request he would offend him. If he granted it he would offend Charles V. He dared not offend Charles, so he temporized. But Henry grew weary of awaiting the pope's pleasure, and he induced Archbishop Cranmer to pronounce the divorce without further appeal to Rome.

Henry VIII Supreme Head of the English Church

Upon this the pope ordered Henry to take back his wife upon pain of excommunication. Instead of obeying, Henry replied by cutting the Church of England free from Rome.

Acts of Parliament were speedily passed declaring that the king of England, and not the pope of Rome, was the supreme head of the English Church, and forbidding the payment of any moneys to the pope. It was also declared that the bishop of Rome had no more jurisdiction in the kingdom

179

of England than any other foreign bishop. Mass was ordered to be said in English instead of in Latin. Masses for the dead, pilgrimages, adoration of relics and images, were forbidden, and the Doctrine of Purgatory was denied. Beyond this Henry made little alteration in the teaching or services of the Church.

He, indeed, suppressed monasteries and convents. But this had nothing to do with religious conviction. He was in need of money, the religious houses were rich in land and money; therefore he suppressed them and took their wealth to himself.

Henry needed an excuse for doing this. His excuse was that the monks and nuns led wicked and idle lives, which were a disgrace to religion. In many cases this was true. Henry, however, did not distinguish between the houses of good or ill repute, but treated all alike. But the monasteries and convents were the hospitals, almshouses, and schools of the day, and the closing of them brought misery on the people. The land, too, was soon filled with homeless, beggared monks, and a rising known as the Pilgrimage of Grace took place. But the rebellion was put down, and Henry continued his suppressions.

Although England was thus separated from Rome not by the zeal of a reformer but by the command of a selfish and stubborn king, king and people were at one. The king's action in breaking with the pope coincided with the wishes of the people; they both girded at papal interference, and both clung to the old theology.

But besides this there was a real desire for reform, and to many it seemed that the king's reform was not radical enough. For many of the people had become imbued with the doctrines of Luther and Calvin, and wished to see England a Protestant country. This was not the king's will. He would brook no opposition to his will, and he put to death impartially Catholics who denied his supremacy as head of the Church, and Protestants who held Calvinistic theories about the Holy Sacrament.

So in England, no more than in other countries, was the Reformation accomplished without bloodshed and persecution. The new English Church persecuted those who refused adherence, but not till Mary Tudor came to the throne did the fires of persecution burn fiercely. She was an ardent Catholic, yet as queen of England she was supreme head of the Anglican Church, a church that she was bound to hate. In her fervent devotion to Rome she endeavoured to bring back England to its allegiance. But in spite of cruel persecution she failed.

Henry VIII had been able to impose his religion on the people of England, because they themselves desired to break with Rome. Mary failed to impose her religion on then, because her will was not theirs. In her blind fealty to Rome she plunged her country into blood. She repealed all the religious legislation of her father and of her brother Edward VI. But all her efforts were in vain. The awakening intellect of England became more and more Protestant and national, and no laws of princes could prevent its final severance from Rome.

John Knox

In Scotland, also, the new religion took root. The great reformer there was John Knox, a follower of Calvin. The success of the Reformation in Scotland was of great importance to the history of Europe. The young queen of Scots, Mary, brought up in France, was heart and soul with the Roman Church. If she had had a united country behind her she might with the help of Rome and France have made good her claim to the throne of England. Then in England the Protestant religion might have been wiped out for ever, even as it was destined to be in France. At least, so it seemed to the politicians of the day. Looking back, it seems very doubtful if the awakened spirit of liberty in England could have been so coerced.

As it was, Scotland was divided between the old religion and the new. English Protestants and Scottish Protestants made common cause against the French and the Catholics, and the allied Protestants triumphed. In this first union of religion may be seen the beginnings of united Britain.

Sweden, Denmark, and Norway

The Reformation spread even to Scandinavia and the far north. There, at first, it was imposed by the rulers somewhat after the manner of the English Reformation. But there, too, the people were ready for reform, and the countries soon became entirely Protestant.

During the centuries when the countries of south-western Europe had been rising to importance, Scandinavia had had little effect on them, and had been little affected by them. Its history is chiefly a record of internal struggles between the three kingdoms of Norway, Sweden, and Denmark for supremacy. In 1397, by the Union of Calmar, these three kingdoms were at length united under one ruler. But still, although they had only one ruler, there was no real union among them.

The Swedes especially hated the domination of Denmark, and more than once tried to regain their independence. Then, in 1520, Christian II of Denmark, in the hope of for ever crushing Swedish independence, massacred all the nobles at Stockholm in cold blood.

This horrible deed was called the Stockholm Bath of Blood, and instead of crushing Sweden's desire for independence it roused the national spirit as it had never been roused before. The Swedes threw off all semblance of allegiance to Denmark, and chose a young noble named Gustavus Vasa for their leader. In 1523 there was a revolution in Denmark. Christian II was driven from the throne, and Gustavus Vasa became king of Sweden, and Frederick I of Holstein king of Denmark and Norway.

With the reign of Gustavus Vasa the history of Sweden as an independent kingdom may be said to begin. But meanwhile the kingdom was wasted with war. The royal treasury was empty, and Gustavus knew not where to turn for money. But although king and people were poor the Church was rich, and Gustavus determined to take the Church revenues for state purposes.

At a meeting of the Diet in 1527 he made clear his intentions. He was met with fierce opposition on the part of the bishops who were present, and finding he could not bend the Diet to his will he rose in anger.

"Then I will no more be your king," he cried, "and if you can find another who will please you better I will rejoice. Pay me for my possessions in the land, give me back what I have spent in your service. Then I shall go. And I swear solemnly I shall never come back to this debased and ungrateful country of mine." And with that he left them.

But the Swedes could not do without Gustavus. It was he alone who held the country together, and in three days they yielded to his demands. Thus by the will of one man the Reformation was established in Sweden.

A little later the Reformation was established in Denmark. Christian II had been attracted to the new religion, and had intended to introduce it, when his subjects had rebelled and driven him from the throne. His successor, Frederick, was a Protestant, and favoured the religion, but it was not until the reign of his son Christian III that it was fully established in the country.

During his reign also the new religion was established in Norway. For unlike Sweden, Norway had failed to assert her independence, and had even lost her old status as a separate kingdom, and become a mere dependency of the kingdom of Denmark.

REFORMATION PERIOD—SPAIN, PORTUGAL, THE NETHERLANDS, AND ITALY

IN Charles V's own kingdom of Spain the Reformation made little impression. This was partly because there was not so much need of it. For the Church there was more alive, and many of the worst abuses rampant in other countries had been removed. But chiefly it was due to the fact that in Spain heresy was promptly and severely suppressed by the terrible Inquisition.

Portugal, too, was hardly touched by the Reformation. For there also the Inquisition was in force, and all individual thought was quickly stamped out by it. Very shortly, too, while Europe was being torn by religious wars Portugal was to become for a time a mere province of Spain. For in 1580 Henry I of Portugal died without heirs, and Philip II of Spain claimed the throne as the heir of his mother Isabella of Portugal. Then for sixty years the kings of Spain ruled Portugal also.

The Inquisition and the Netherlands

In the Netherlands, which were at this time not an independent country but merely the private possession of Charles, the Reformation brought bloodshed, persecution, and war. There the struggle for religious freedom was combined with the struggle for political freedom. In the end both were won. Holland became independent of Spain, and one of the strongest Protestant powers in Europe. But that day had not yet dawned. In the meantime Charles determined to do what he liked with his personal property.

The Reformation had taken a great hold upon the Netherlands. Even from quite early days the people had never been very submissive to the pope. Heresy easily took root there, and in spite of horrible persecutions grew and flourished. Long before the Reformation the land swarmed with Wycliffites, Hussites, Waldenses, and adherents of many other dissenting sects. When at length the great Reformation came, with its ally the printing-press, it took root in the Netherlands and spread more rapidly than in any other place.

But Charles was a politician. He well understood that religious

184

liberty was the forerunner of political liberty, and he determined to stamp out the new religion. So the Inquisition was introduced. The reading of the Bible was forbidden, as were also all gatherings for devotion or religious discussion. But the stolid, industrious people resisted. Hundreds and thousands were tortured and put to death. Still the adherents of the new religion increased, persecution only making them more determined to walk in the way upon which they had set their feet. It was left for the heirs of Charles to reap the harvest he had sown, and Holland was lost alike to Spain, to the Empire, and to the pope.

Italy and the Reformation

In Italy, divided as it was at this time between the rule of the pope and the rule of Spain, the Reformation made considerable headway. Italians lived beneath the shadow of the papacy, they were nearer than others to the fountain of evil, and many devout men longed to see the Church made pure and holy. There was, too, a great deal of intercourse between Germany and Italy. Both scholars and merchants constantly crossed the Alps, and Luther's doctrines soon found many sympathizers among Italians. But in Italy, as in Spain, the reform movement was rigorously repressed. The Inquisition did its work thoroughly, and Italy remained within the fold of the Church.

Broadly speaking then, when the Reformation had worked itself out, the whole of north-western Europe, the half of Christendom, was lost to the papacy. England, Scotland, Norway, Sweden, Denmark, Holland, northern Germany, and part of Switzerland had adopted the new religion in one form or another. Italy, Spain, Portugal, Ireland, and, in the long run, France, with portions of southern Germany, clung to the old religion.

The Reformation did not bring complete freedom of religious thought or real toleration. For the reformers merely changed an infallible Church for an infallible Bible. Each reformer, Luther, Zwingli, or Calvin produced his own dogma, and would admit of no salvation for those who differed from him. So there arose countless divisions among the Protestants, divisions which did much to check their further progress.

The reformers fought and died for freedom of conscience. But they permitted no freedom to those who differed from themselves, and one Protestant sect, when it had the power, was as ready to persecute another as the older church had been. Still, the principle of the right of private judgment had been admitted. It could not again be denied, and even more than in what it did the value of the Reformation lies in the fact that it made possible, and prepared the way for, modern toleration.

The Counter-Reformation: Ignatius Loyola

It also reformed and purified the Church of Rome. As country after country revolted, the ancient Church awoke from her sloth of centuries, resolved to make an end of the evils which had made her a reproach and a byword, and the Counter-Reformation began. In 1545 the Council of Trent was called, and a plain restatement of the Church's doctrines was made. Many causes of stumbling to devout Catholics were removed, and henceforth no man of evil life has sat upon the throne of St. Peter.

This Counter-Reformation stayed the force of the reformers even more than the dissensions among Protestants. To remain at peace within the Church purified was all that many a devout Catholic asked. And soon the Church found a powerful helper in Ignatius Loyola, a Spaniard, who, in 1540, founded the Society of Jesus. The aim of this society was to defend the Church and spread its doctrines. Soon its well-disciplined, scholarly, and devoted members were to be found all over the world. And to them the Church owed much of its re-established authority.

After the Reformation the borders of the ancient Church were doubtless narrowed. Yet in a sense it was stronger than it had been for centuries. Once again its prelates showed to the world the beauty of holiness, and by godly living made for the Church a bulwark against further assaults from without or from within.

Yet religious freedom was by no means won. Europe was divided into two hostile camps. Neither side had as yet learned toleration of the other, and for long years the wars which shook the continent were wars of religion.

THE EFFECT OF AMERICAN
CONQUESTS ON SPAIN

THE reign of Charles V was the age of Spanish conquest and domination in America. This conquest had a great effect first on Spain and ultimately on Europe. For Spain was the first European nation to found an overseas empire. Yet it was no empire in the modern sense of the word. Mexico, Peru, and Chili were explored and exploited, but they were not colonized as we understand the word. The conquerors did not reclaim or cultivate the land. Indeed, they were actually forbidden to grow vines or grain in the conquered countries, lest Spanish trade in wine and corn should be injured.

They were also forbidden to emigrate and settle there. For Spain, far from requiring an outlet for superfluous population, was already too thinly populated, foreign wars being a constant drain upon its manhood. Emigration, therefore, instead of being a necessity, was an actual menace.

The Spaniards, at the same time, were intensely jealous of their overseas trade. They tried to keep it entirely for themselves, and shut out not only all other European nations but even all Spain except Castile. This produced smuggling and piracy on an enormous scale. And soon the proud galleons of Spain, which at one time could sail the seas in safety, were obliged to go in companies to avoid the attack of pirates.

All the Spaniards did then was to procure as much gold and silver from these lands as they could. And this they procured not by their own toil but by the forced labour of the natives whom they had enslaved. Soon gold and silver poured into Spain. It was from America that Charles drew much of the wealth which enabled him to carry on his many wars. With that wealth at command he might have succeeded in dominating Europe, and in founding the world empire he desired to found, but for one thing which wrecked all his plans. This was the Reformation. By it his policy was divided, his alliances complicated, his great ambitions baffled. Thus, for him, in a manner the conquest of America and the Reformation annulled each other.

But although gold and silver poured into Spain from the New World,

Spain became no richer. For the Spaniards spent this easily won wealth like water. Most of it went out of Spain again to pay for the hire of foreign soldiers, and for foreign luxuries, which the Spaniard could no longer do without. For Spain had no manufactures, and as its population constantly lessened in numbers even agriculture was neglected.

At length the country could not grow enough corn and wine to supply the demand of its own people, and foreign merchants supplied these things. So the enormous wealth of America profited Spain not at all. The country gradual grew poorer. Noble beggary became the fashion. The Spaniard, born generous and grown proud, disdained to toil, and the labour in field and workshop was left to foreigners. Their labours again brought Spain no profit, for having made their fortunes they returned home carrying their wealth with them.

Thus once again seeking to dominate Europe a great ruler cast his own kingdom down from the high place she had won. With both hands the Spaniards flung away the golden prize which their daring seamen had wrested from the ocean, and the New World became the heritage of another race.

While the mother-country declined the colonies could not prosper. Under the inhuman treatment of their conquerors the native populations of these colonies dwindled, and a bitter hatred grew up between them and their masters. Charles, indeed, took some interest in his American possessions, and even tried to make good laws for them. But he was too much preoccupied by his efforts to dominate Europe to make much headway. He knew little of the principles of commerce, and he was utterly ignorant of the modern ideas of colonization, the Cortes, or parliament, equally so. Consequently the dealings of Spain with her overseas possessions is a record of mistakes and lost opportunities.

www.ingramcontent.com/pod-product-compliance
Lightning Source LLC
LaVergne TN
LVHW030633080426
835509LV00022B/3456

* 9 7 8 1 6 4 7 9 9 9 4 9 0 *